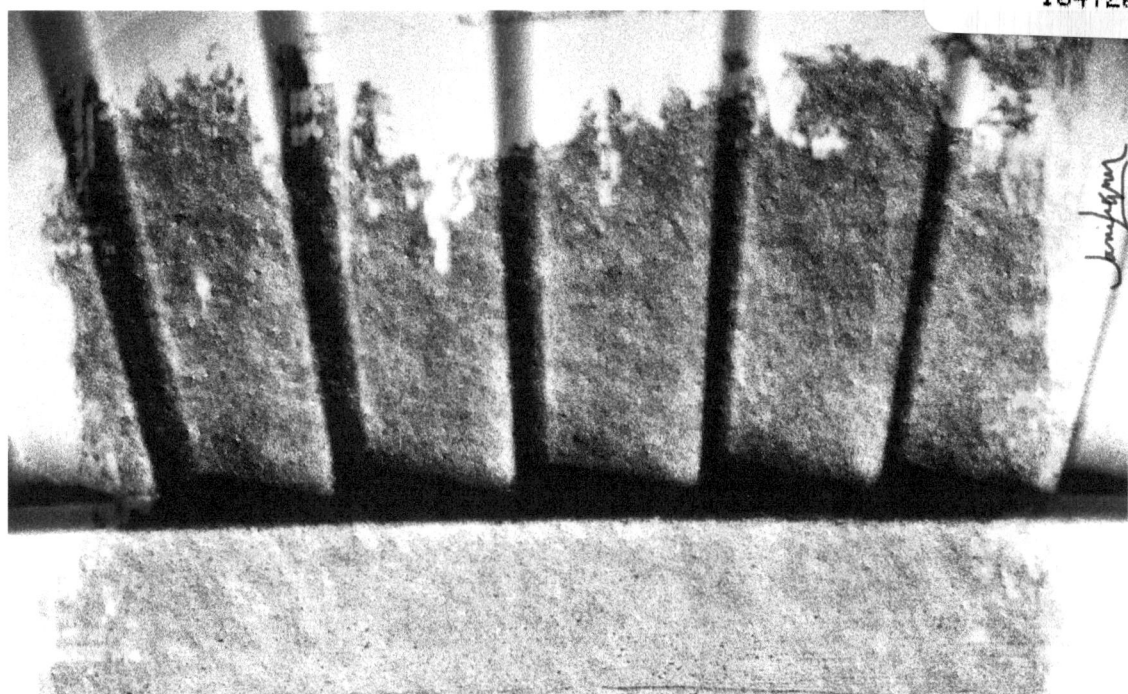

The Eye Behind The Lense

Photography of Janie Lynn Johnson

Original Photography by: Janie Lynn Johnson

Compiled by: Jason Koba

New Jersey : Sound Impressions : 2012

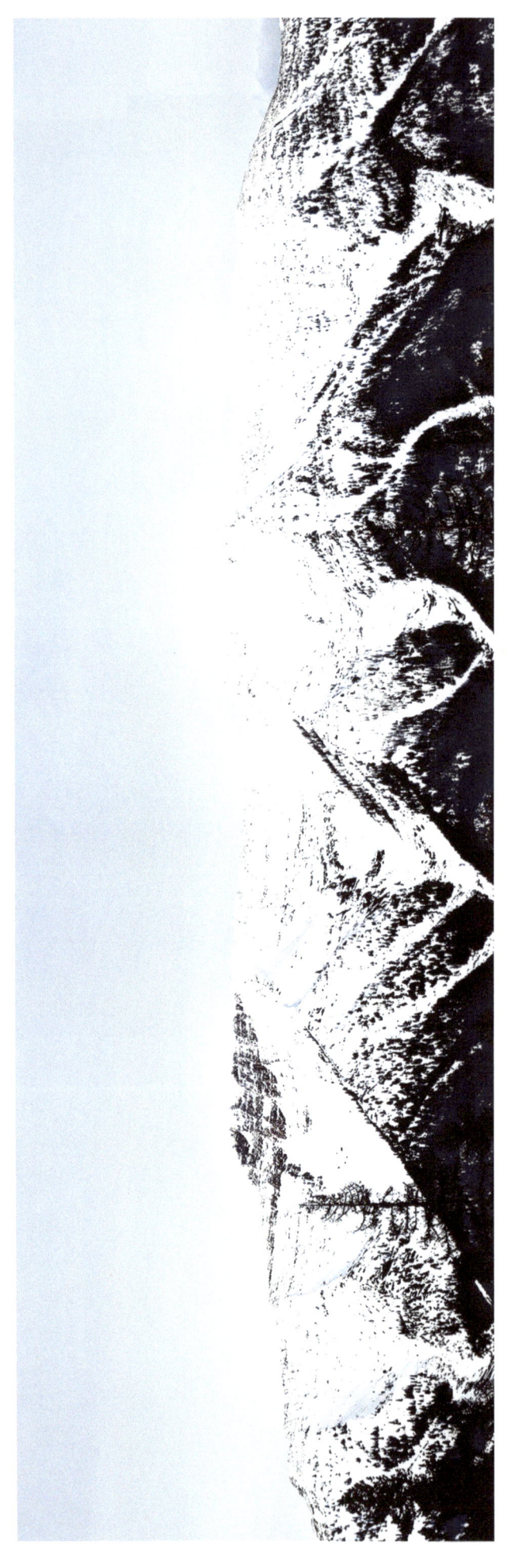

I want to dedicate this book to my three children- Kyra, Andrew, and Carter Connell (they mean the world to me and our relationship with each other only grows stronger with each passing day. Just as I have always stood by them with love and support, they have always done the same for me and I couldn't be any more proud of that and wouldn't trade them for the world) and to my late grandfather Ted Merseal (for helping me to pursue my dream of photography).

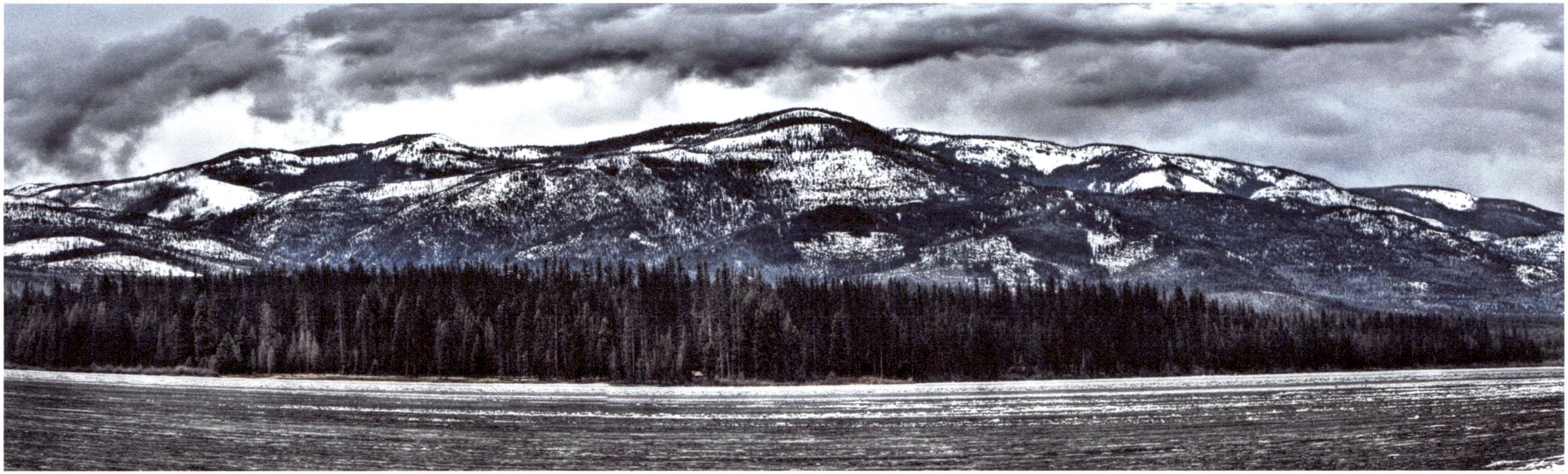

I give thanks to Jason Koba -my dearest friend who is always there for me, my kids, and my father for believing so much in me and giving me so much support in my passion to create and in life. I want to especially give thanks to a friend a long the way who opened my eyes to the beauty and the wonder in life and help me realize my dreams, my true potential, and giving me the confidence to stand proud and not let anyone or any obstacle prevent me from being who I am and showing what I have to offer. I also give thanks to all my family, for if it wasn't for them I would not be the person I am today. Thank you all and god bless. - Janie Lynn

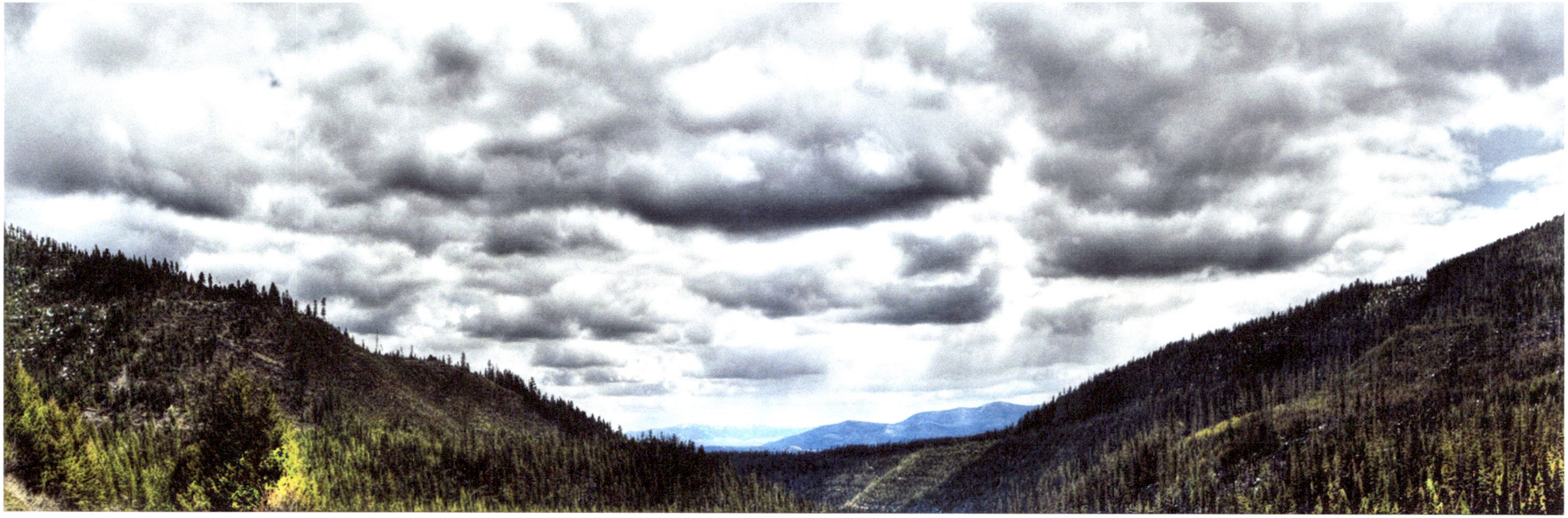

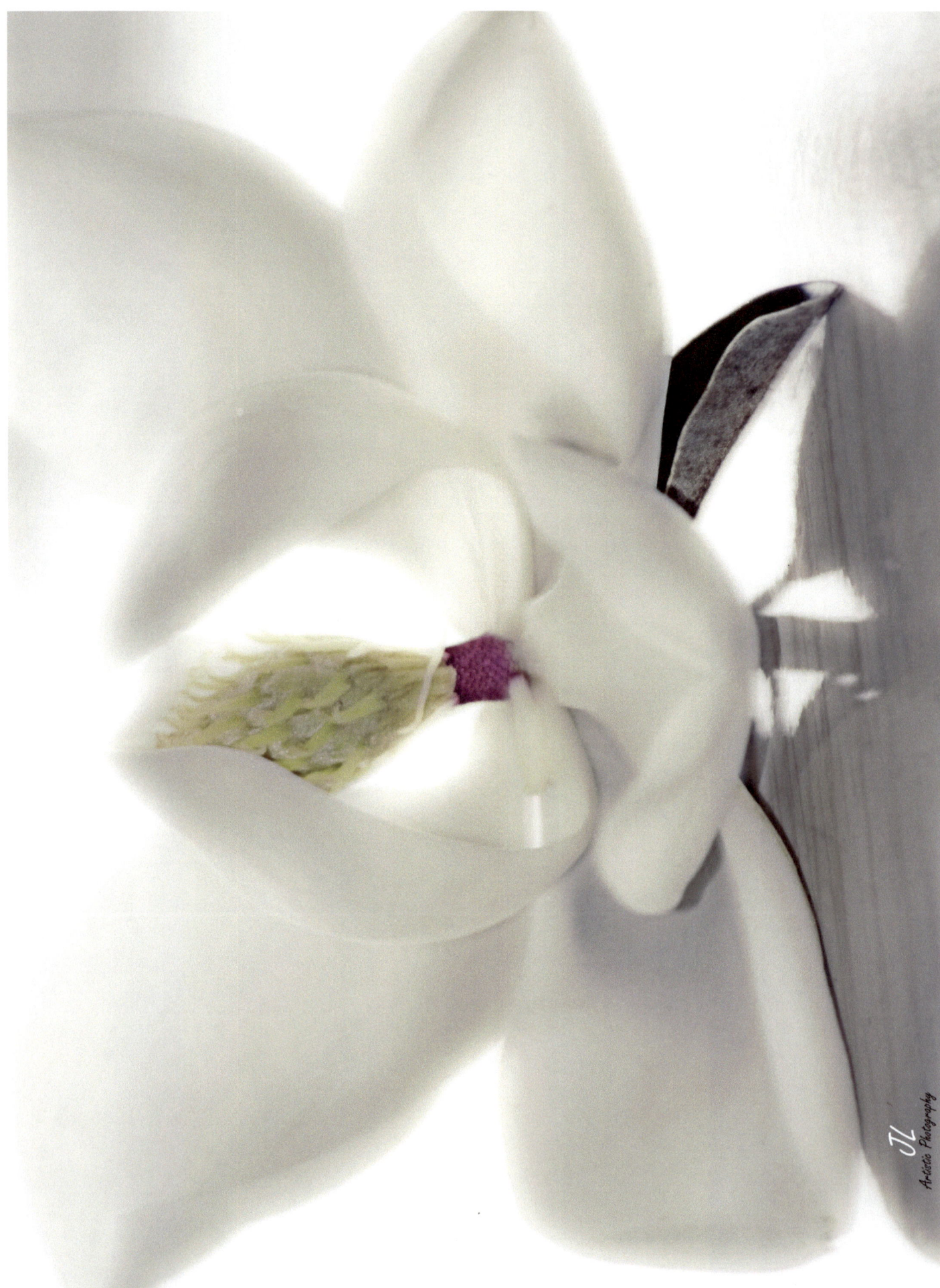

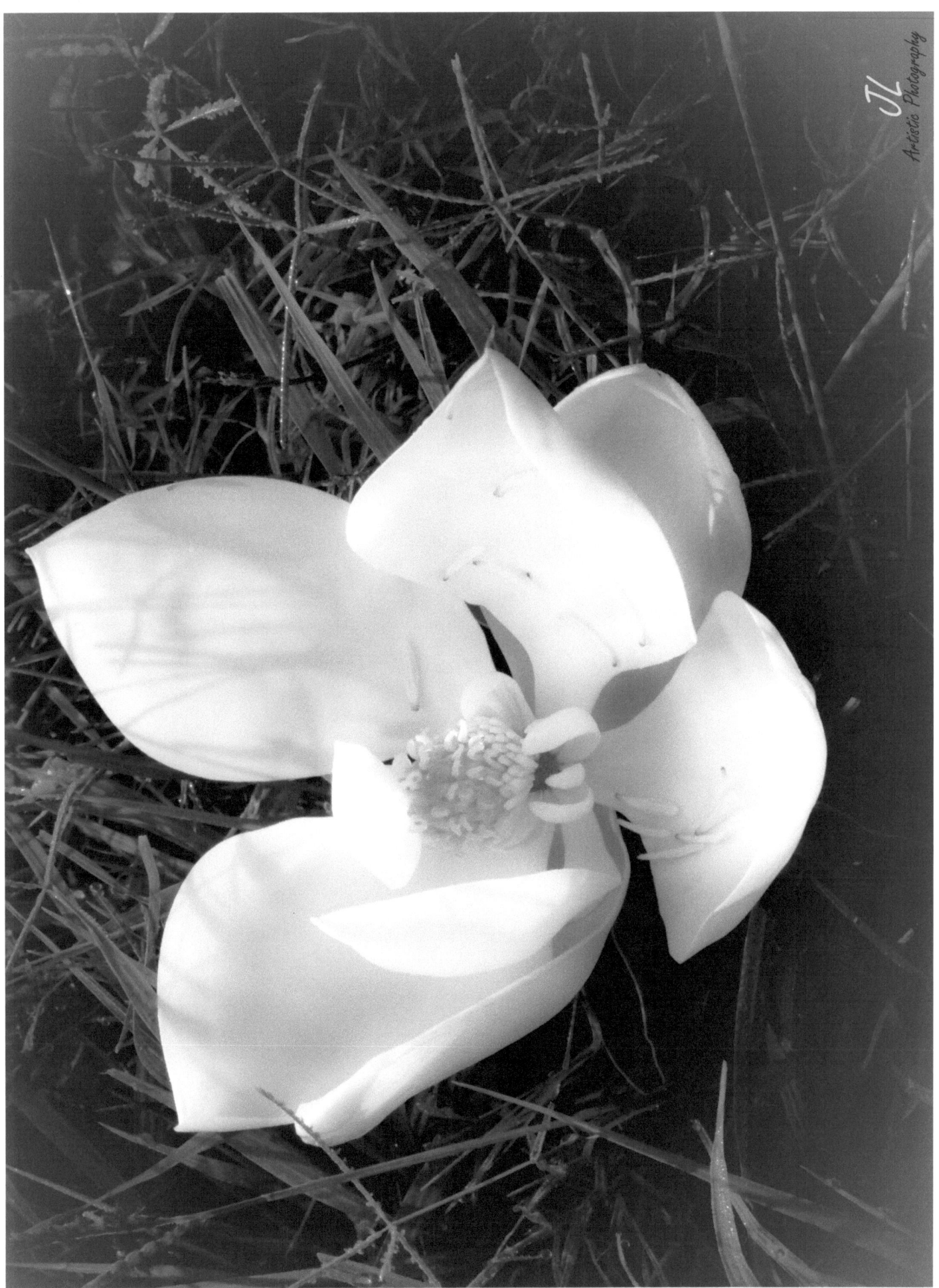

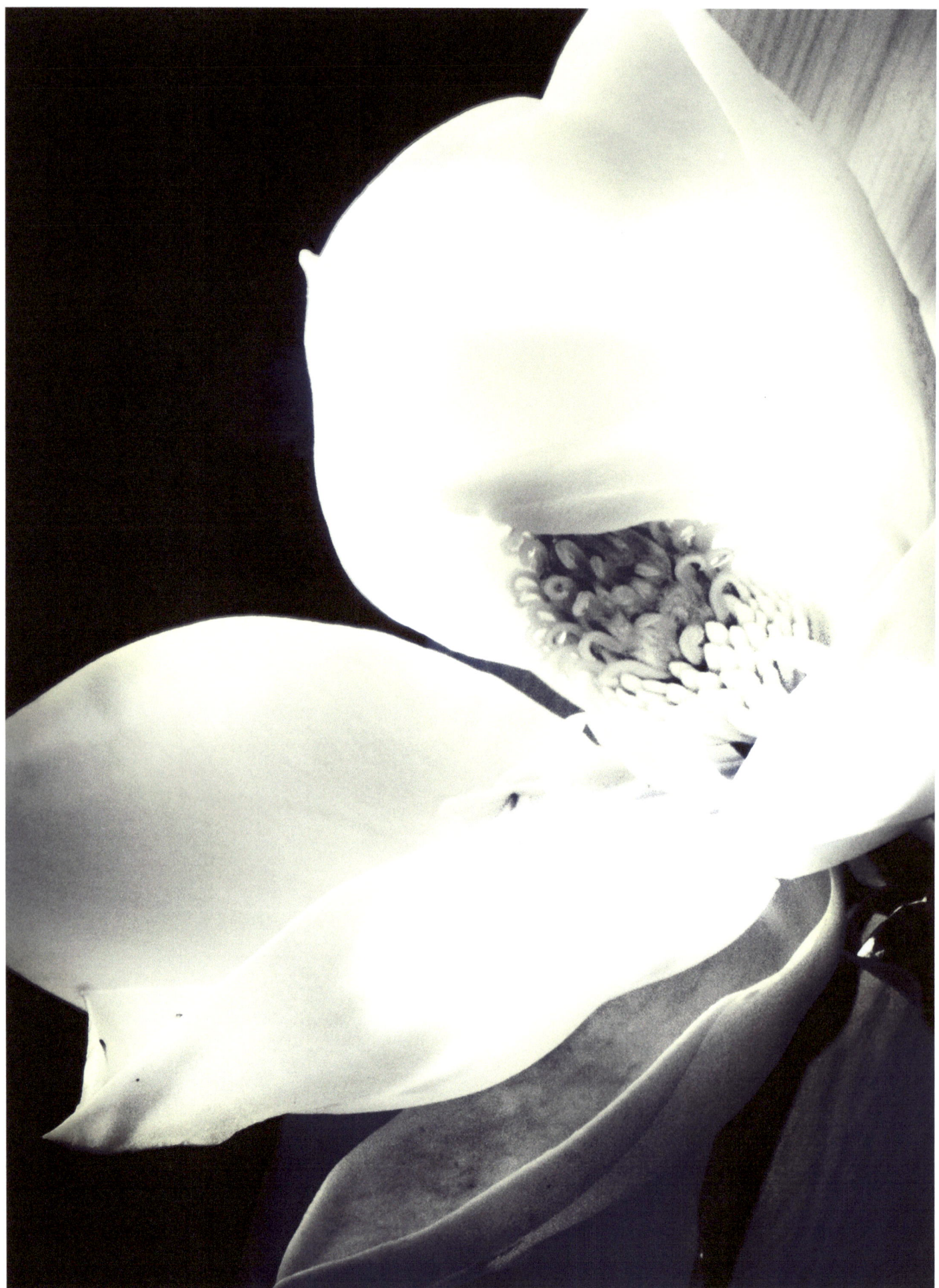

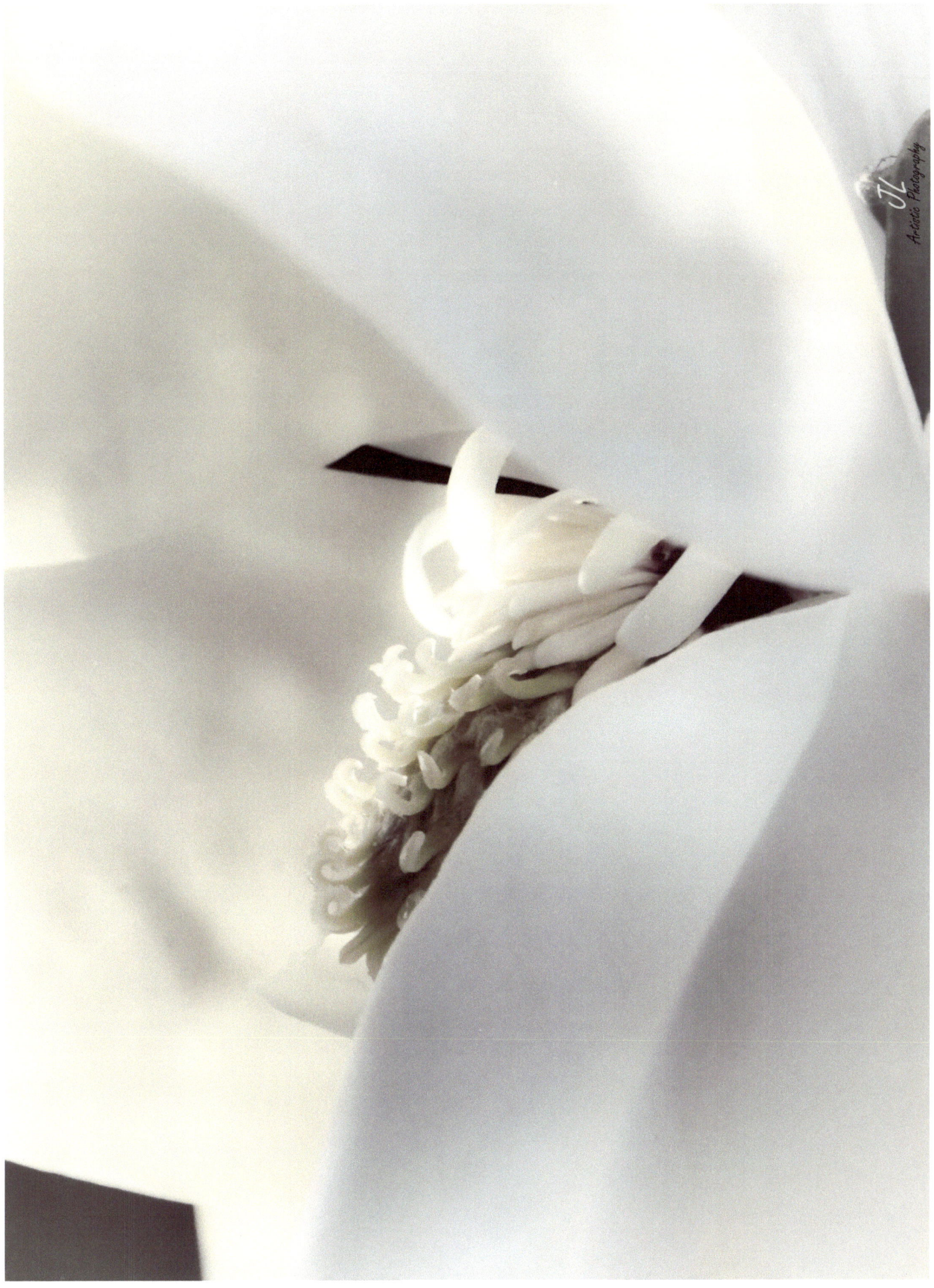

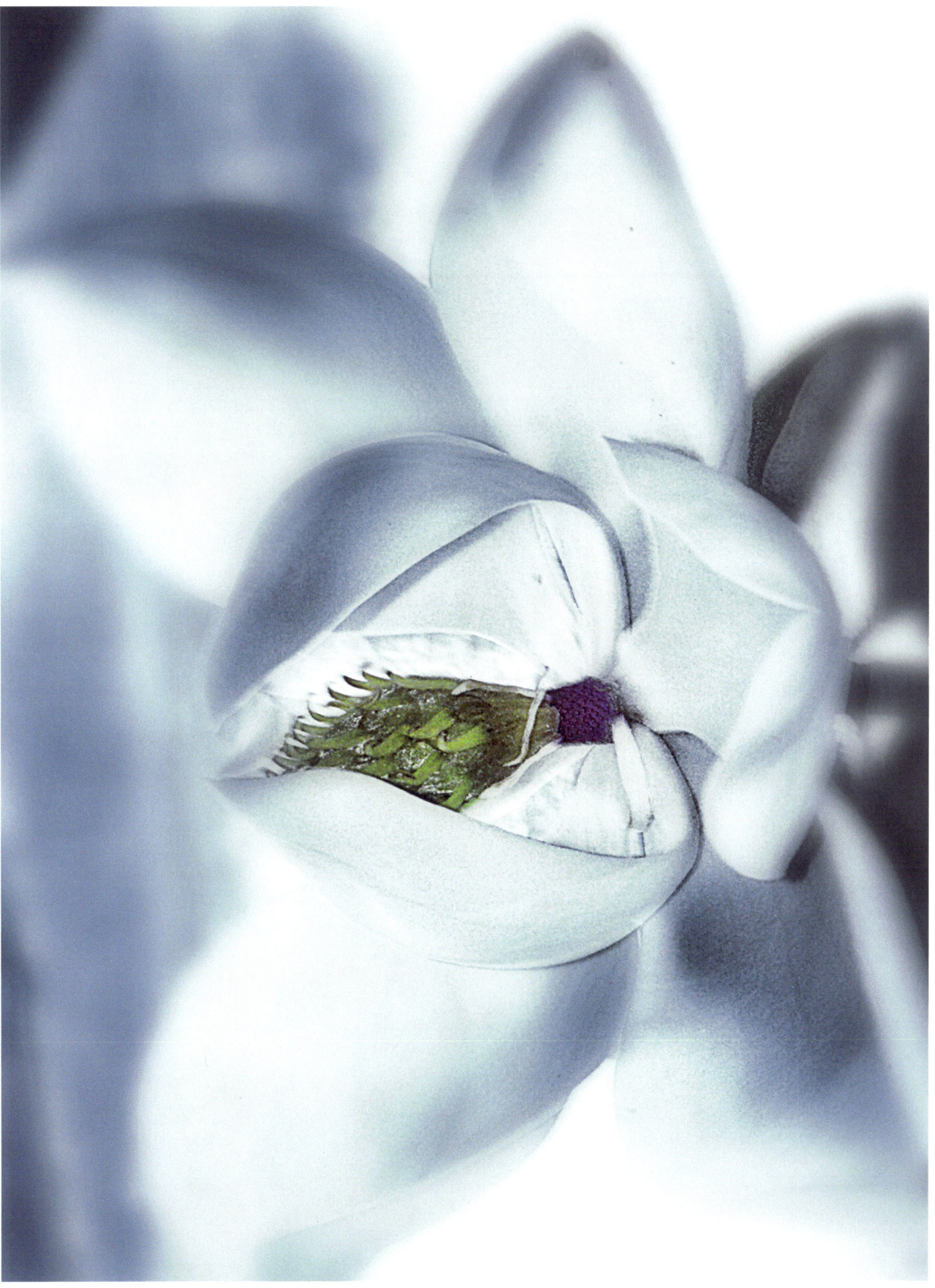

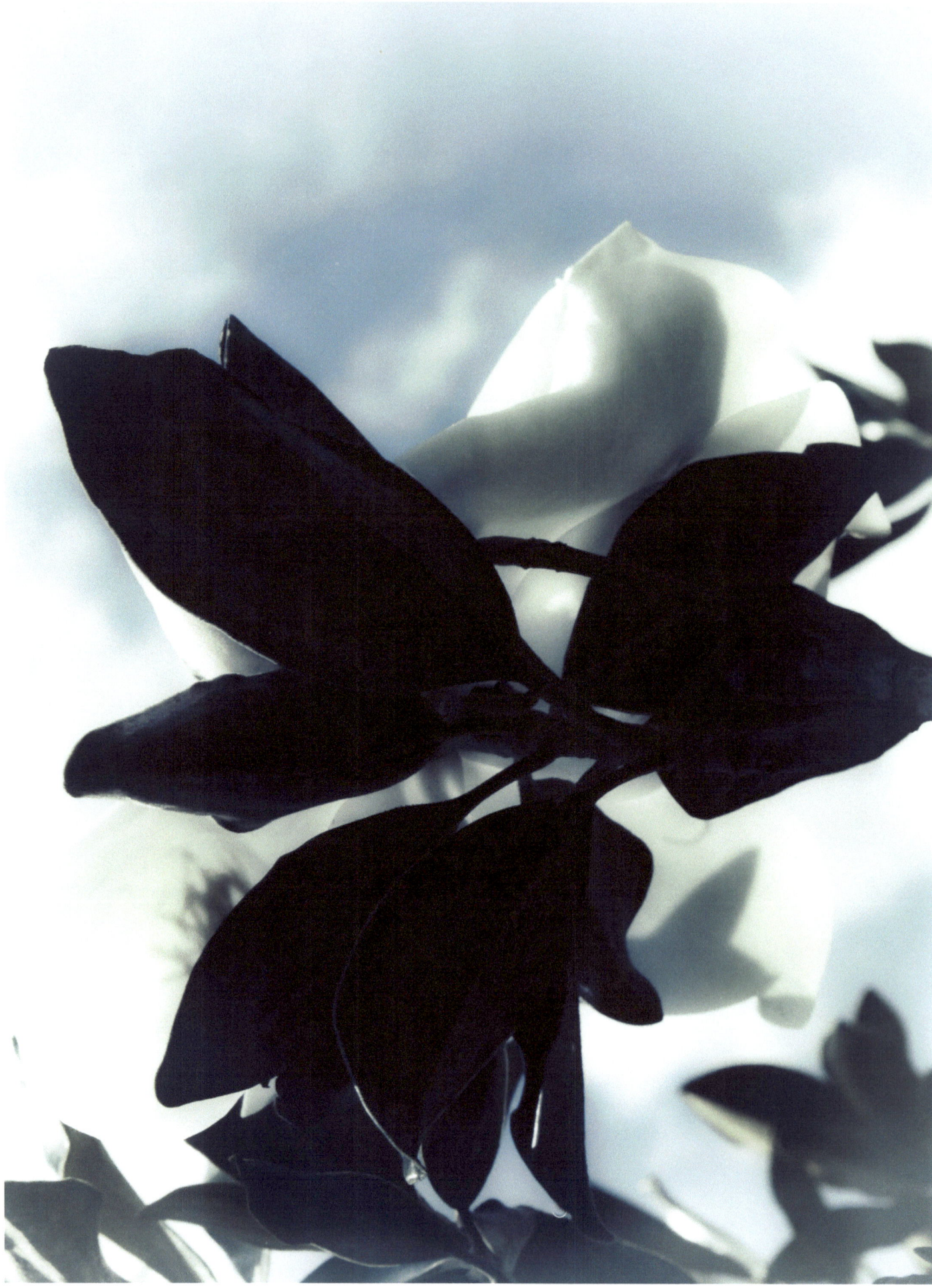

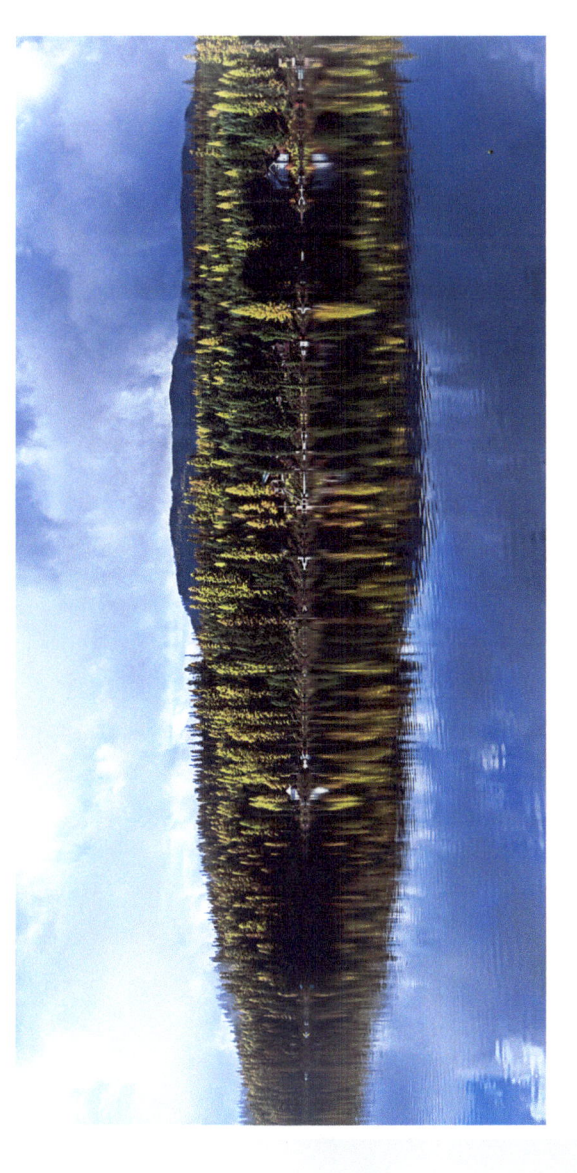

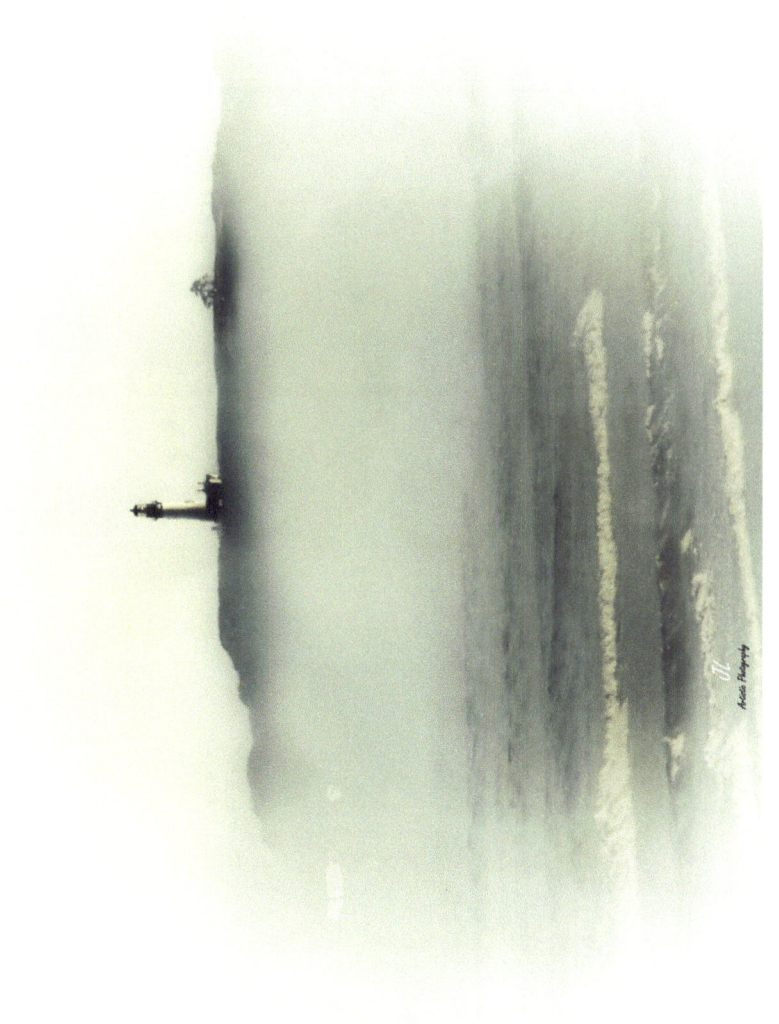

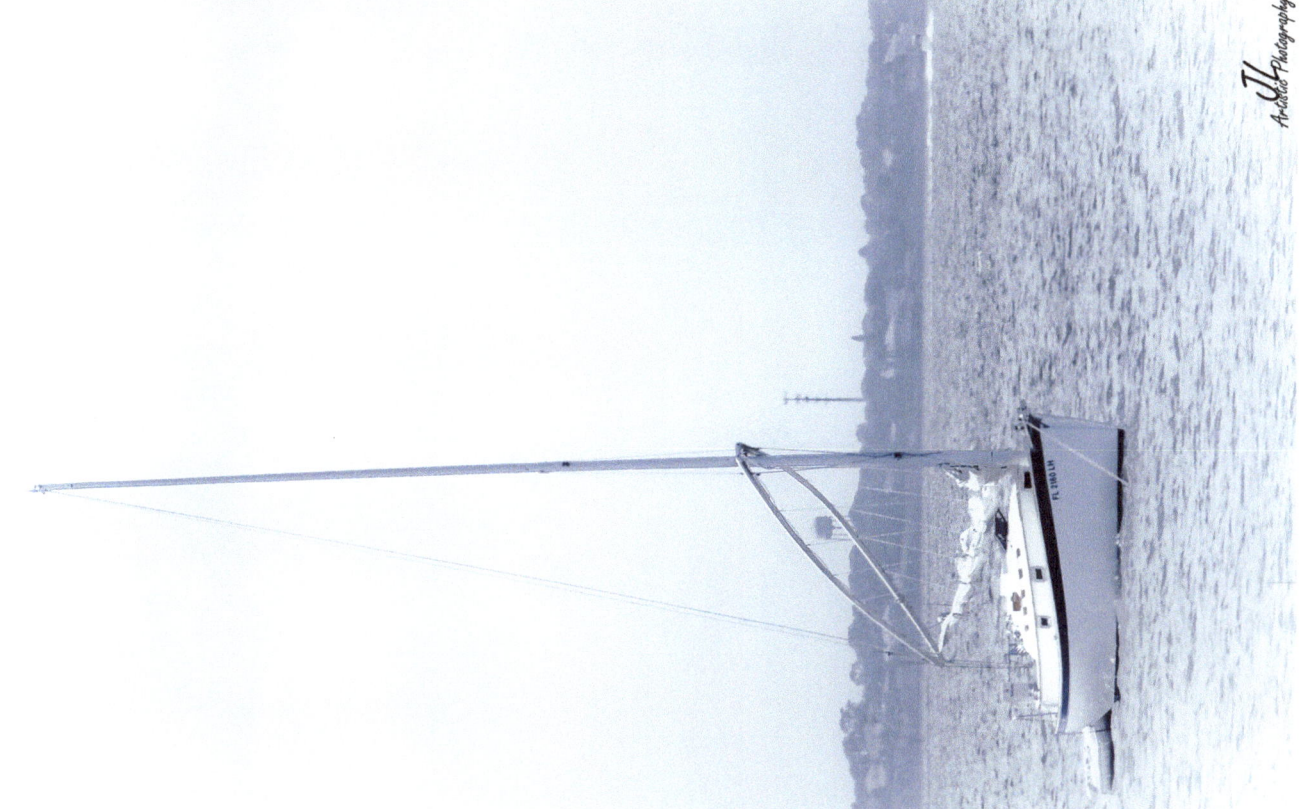

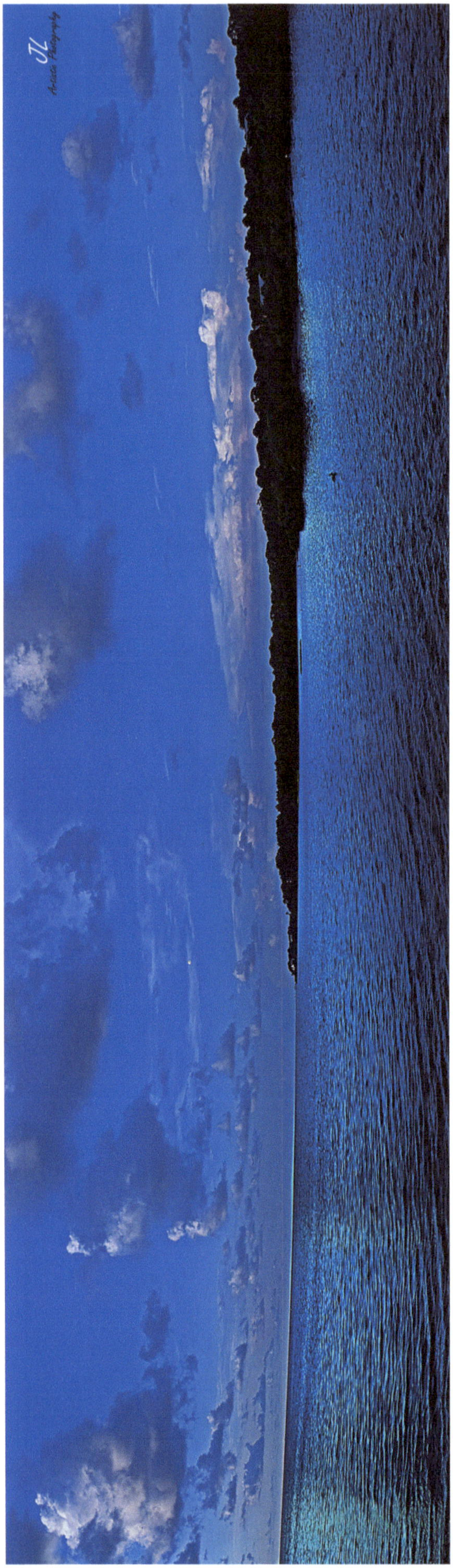

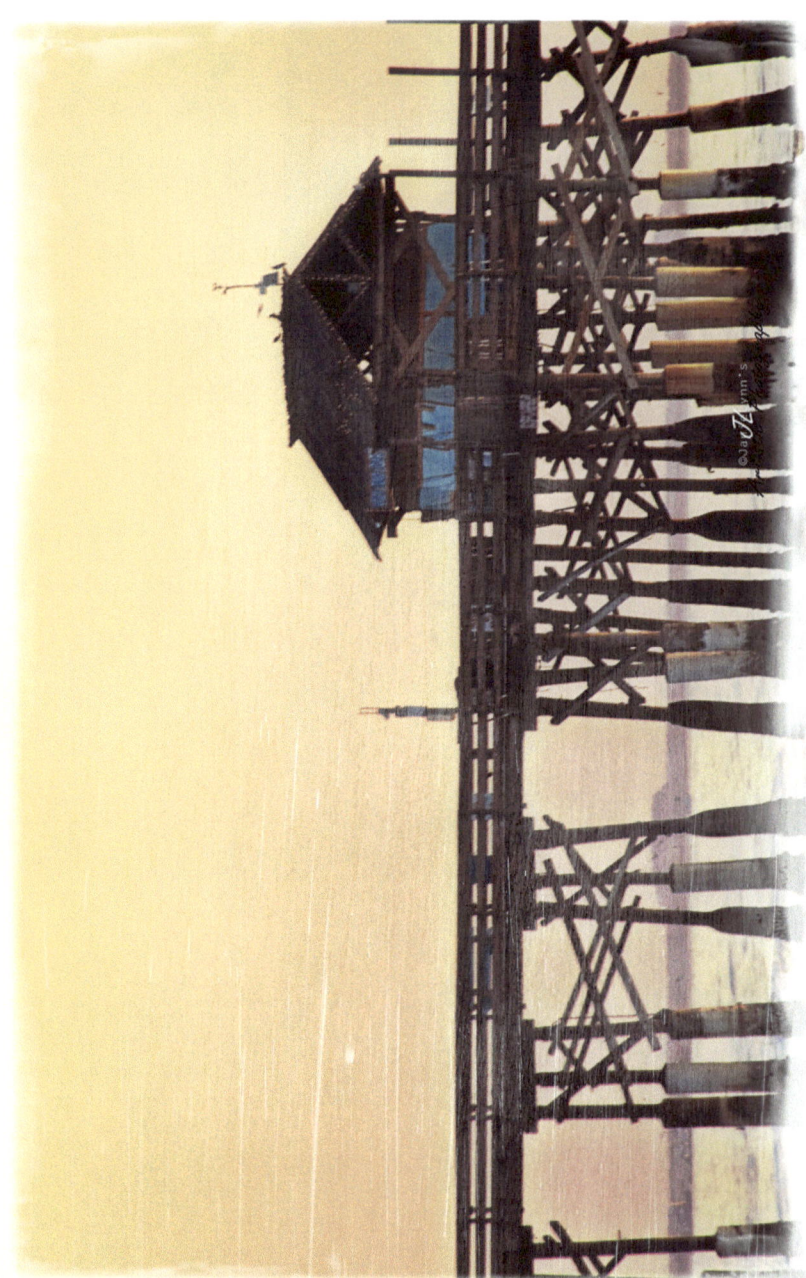
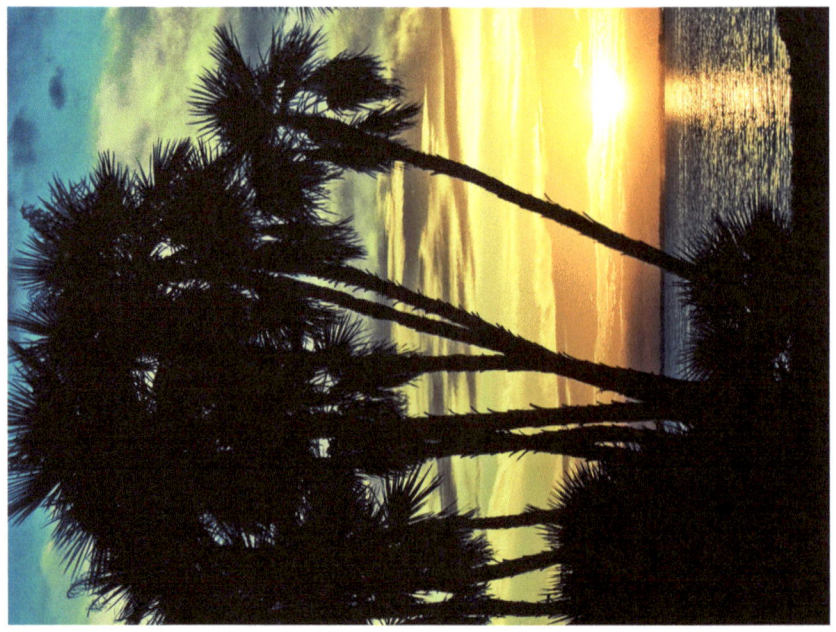

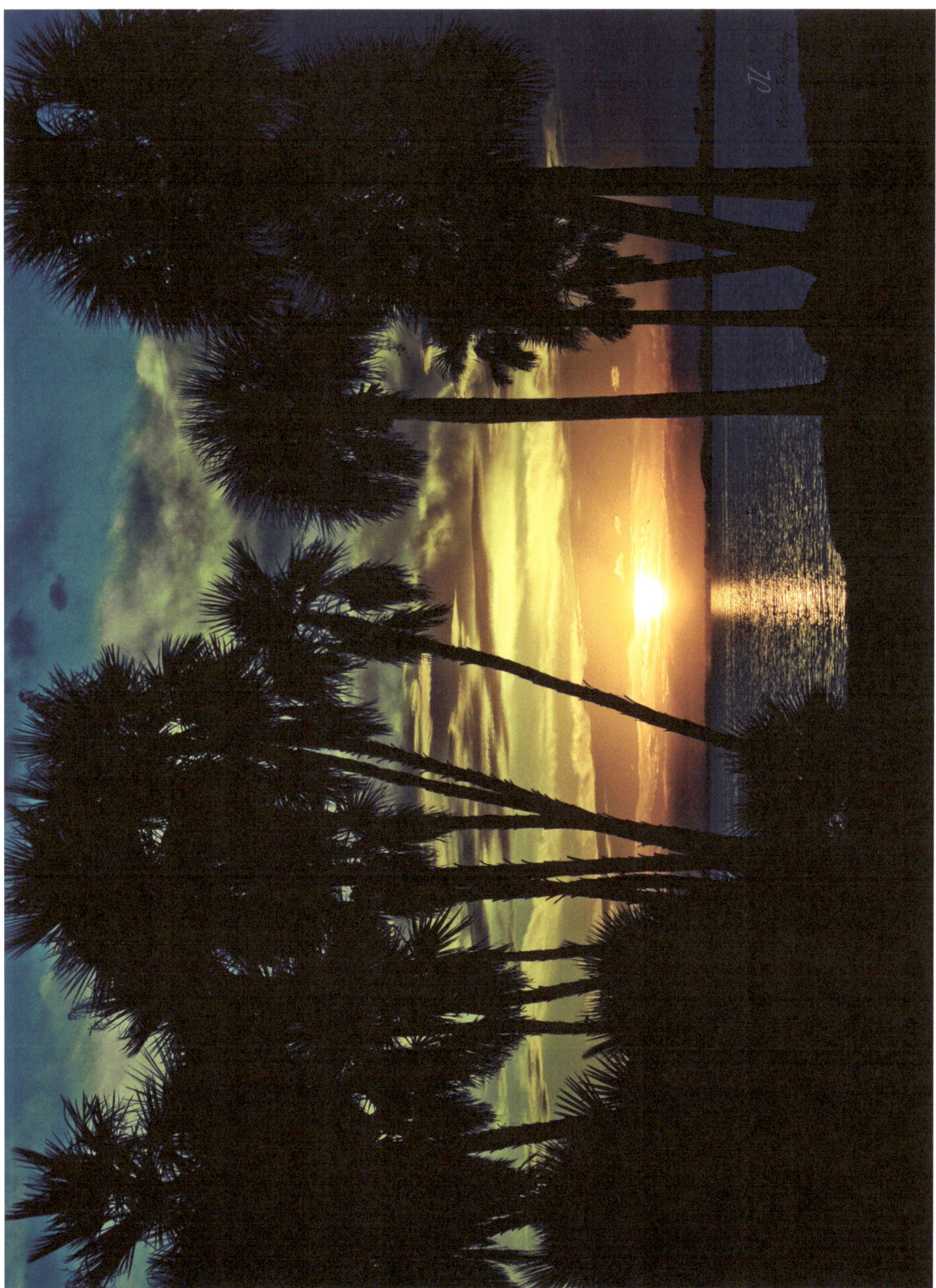

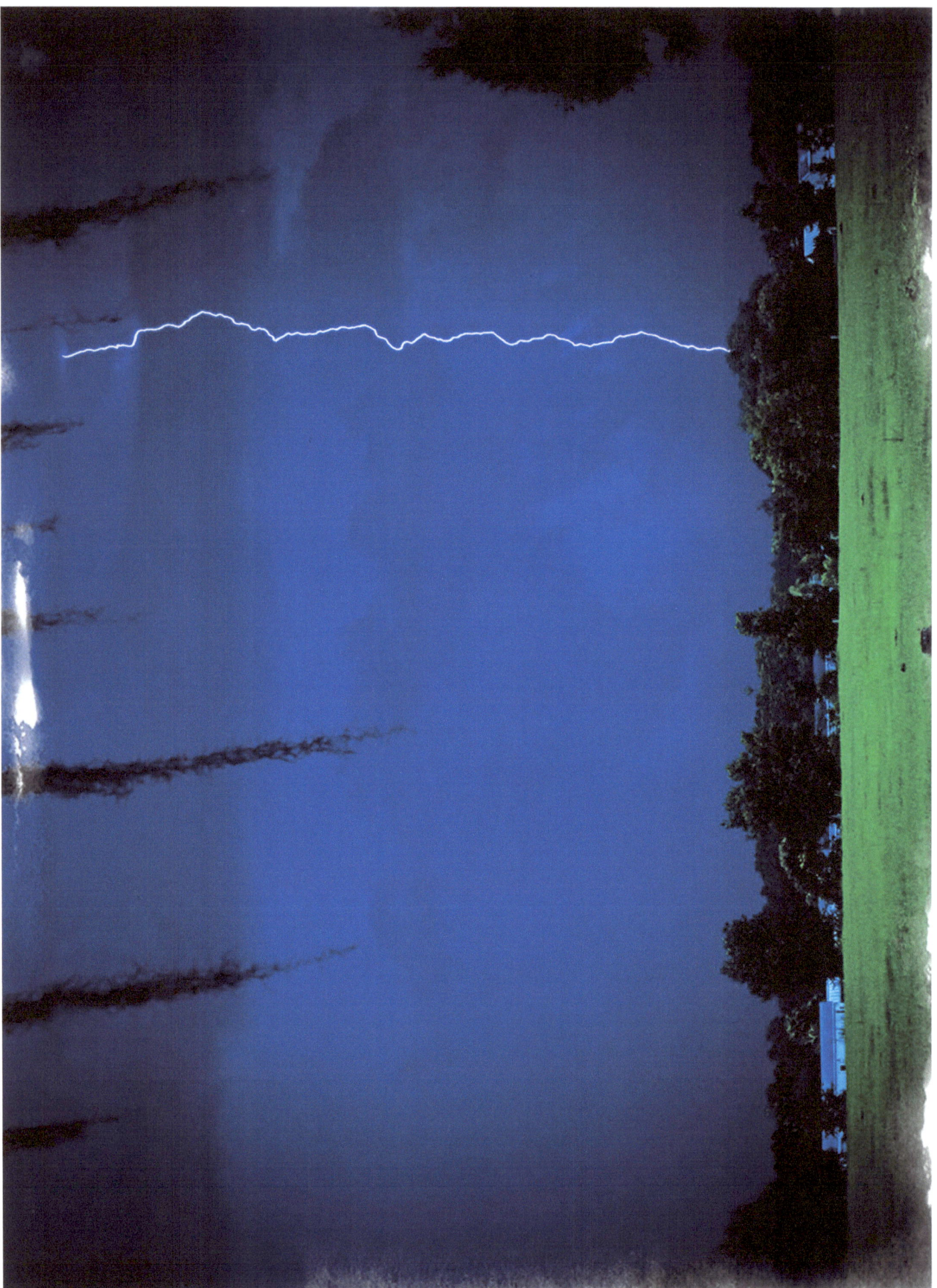

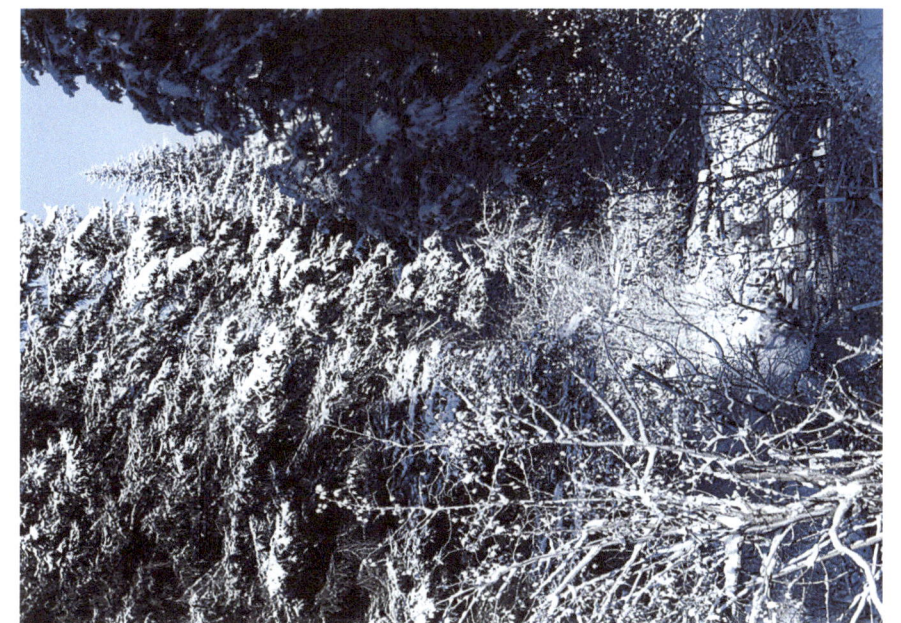

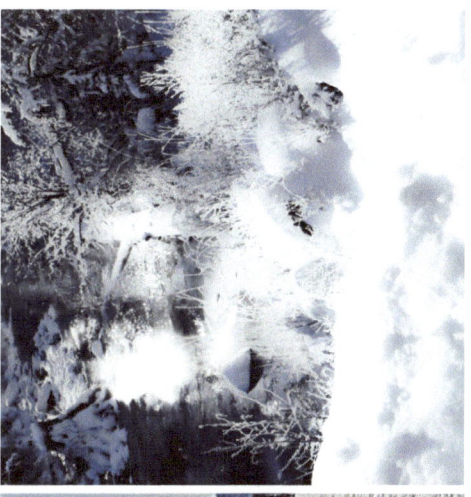

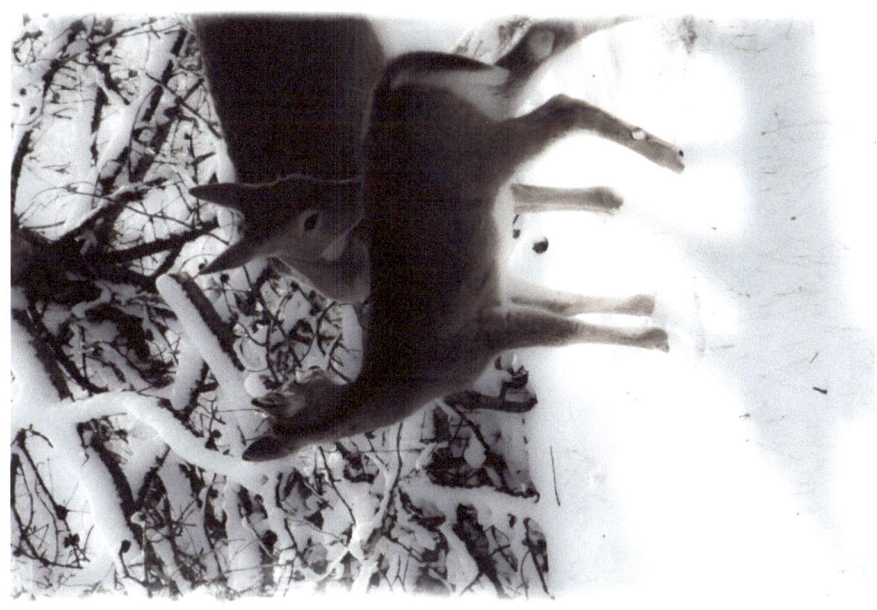

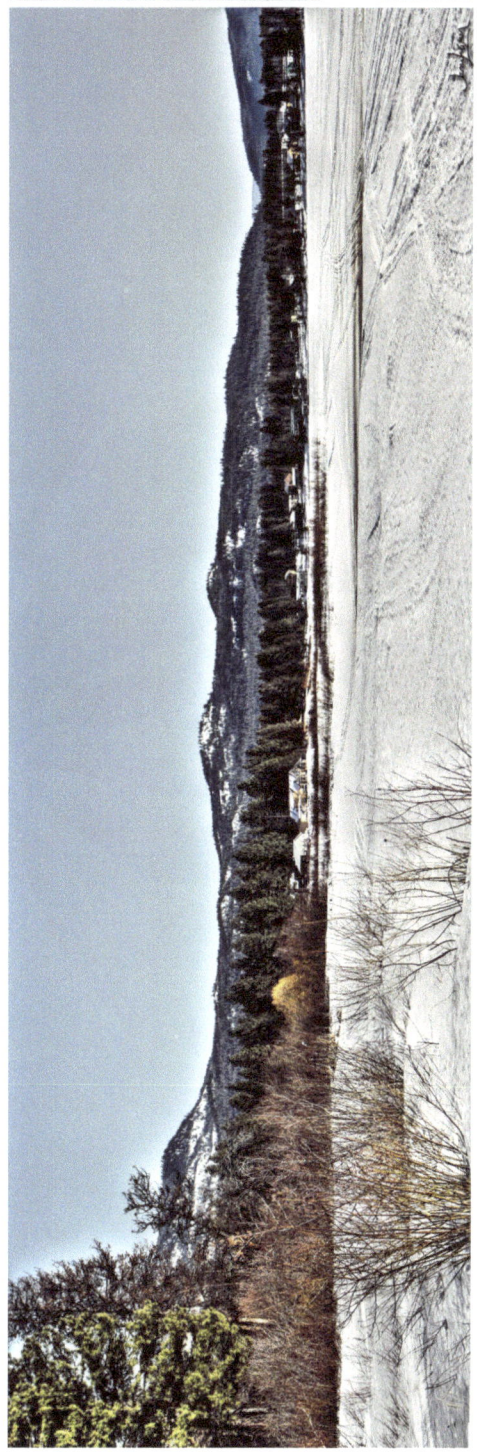

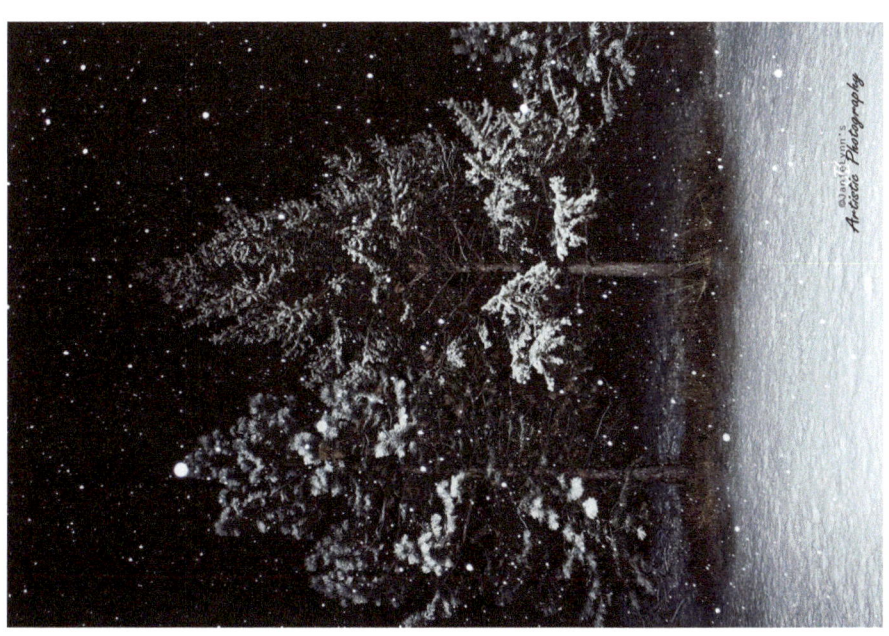

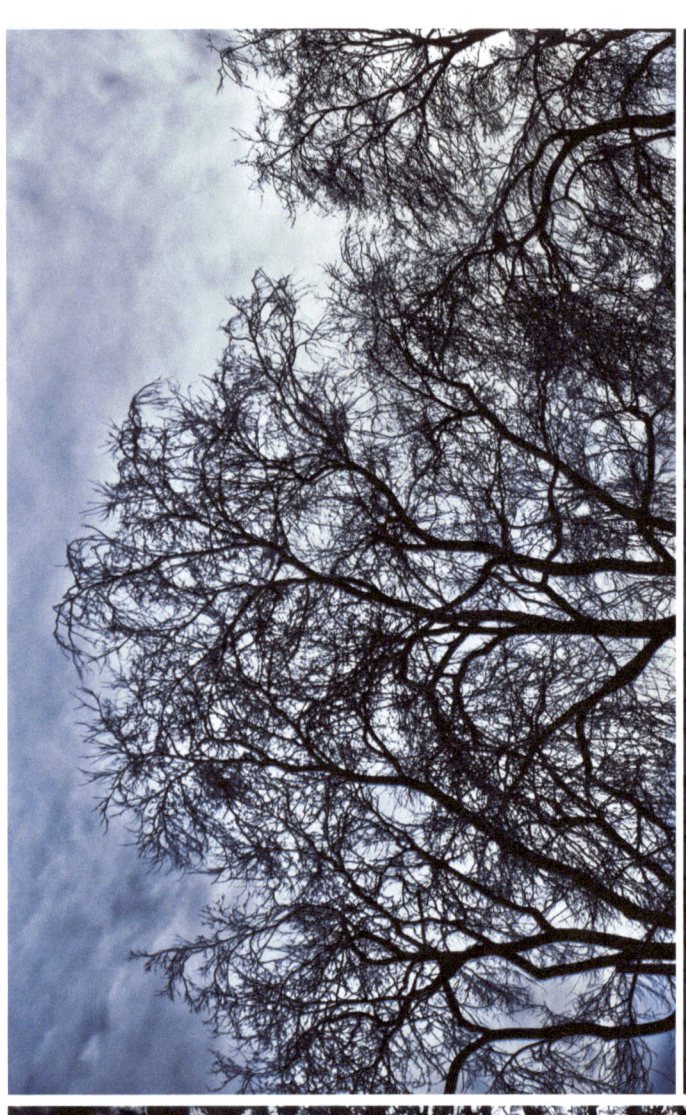
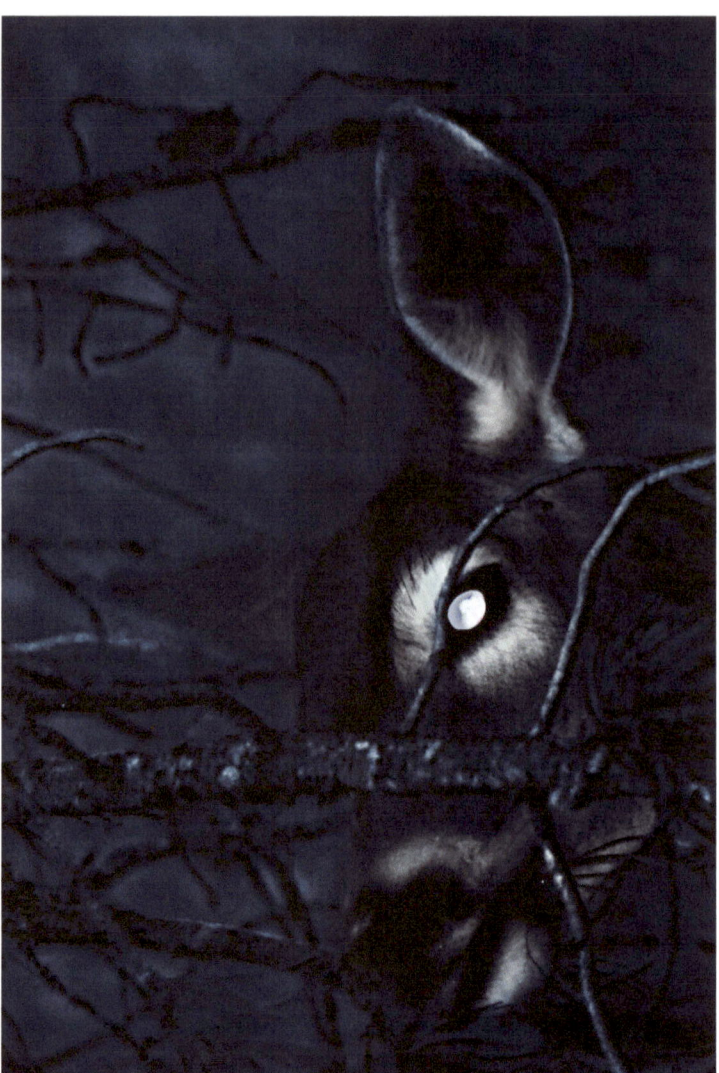

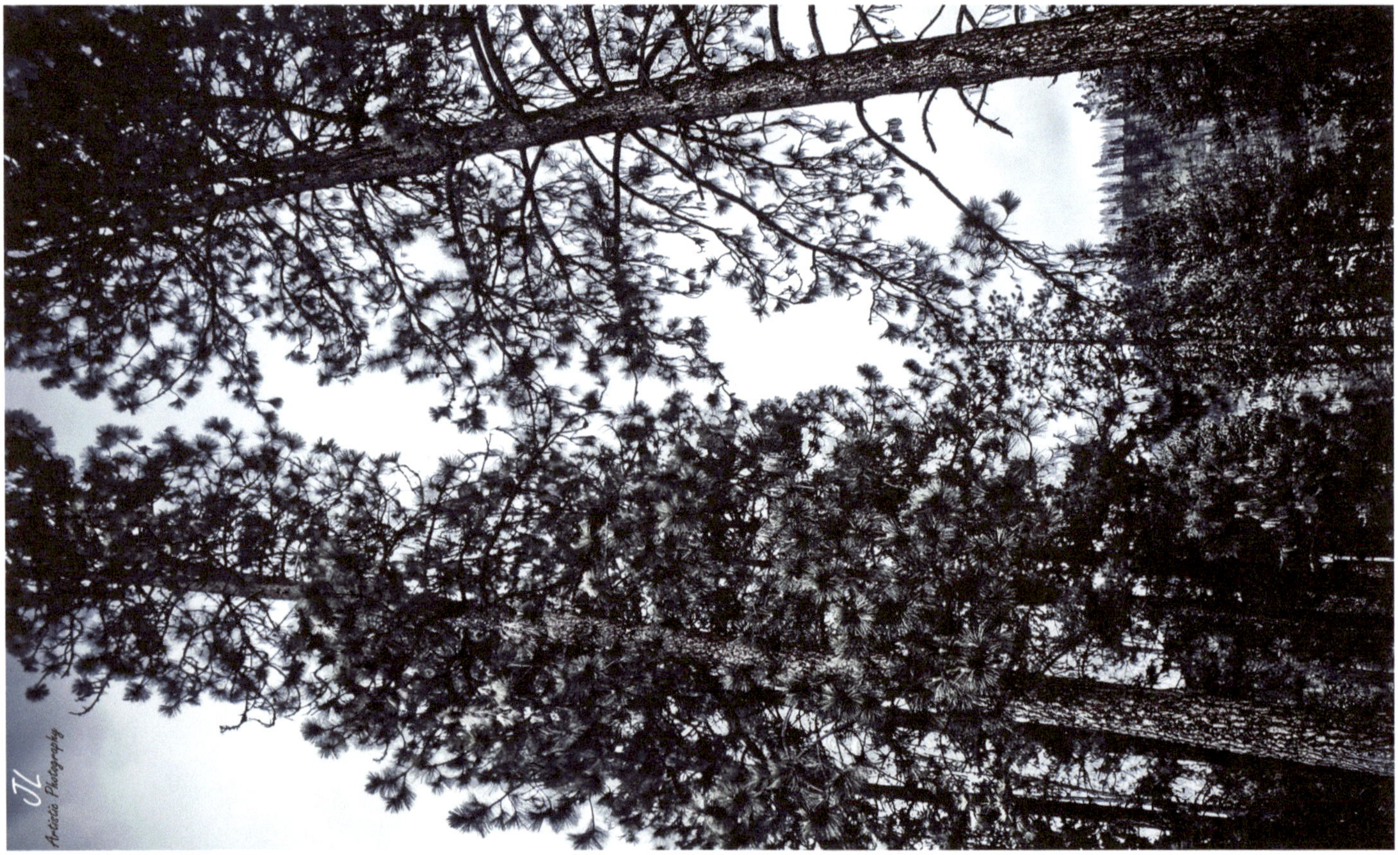

JL
Artisia Photography

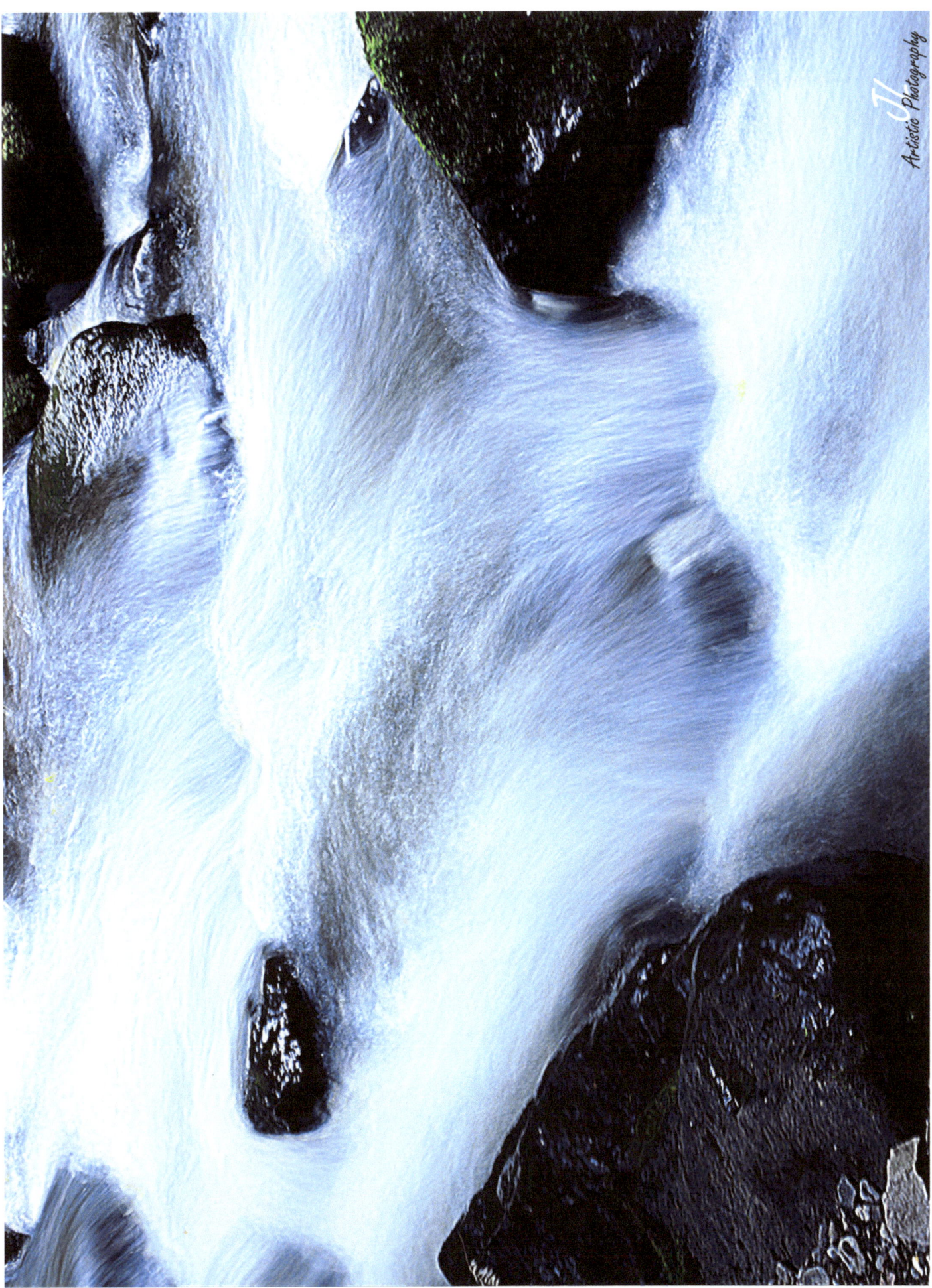

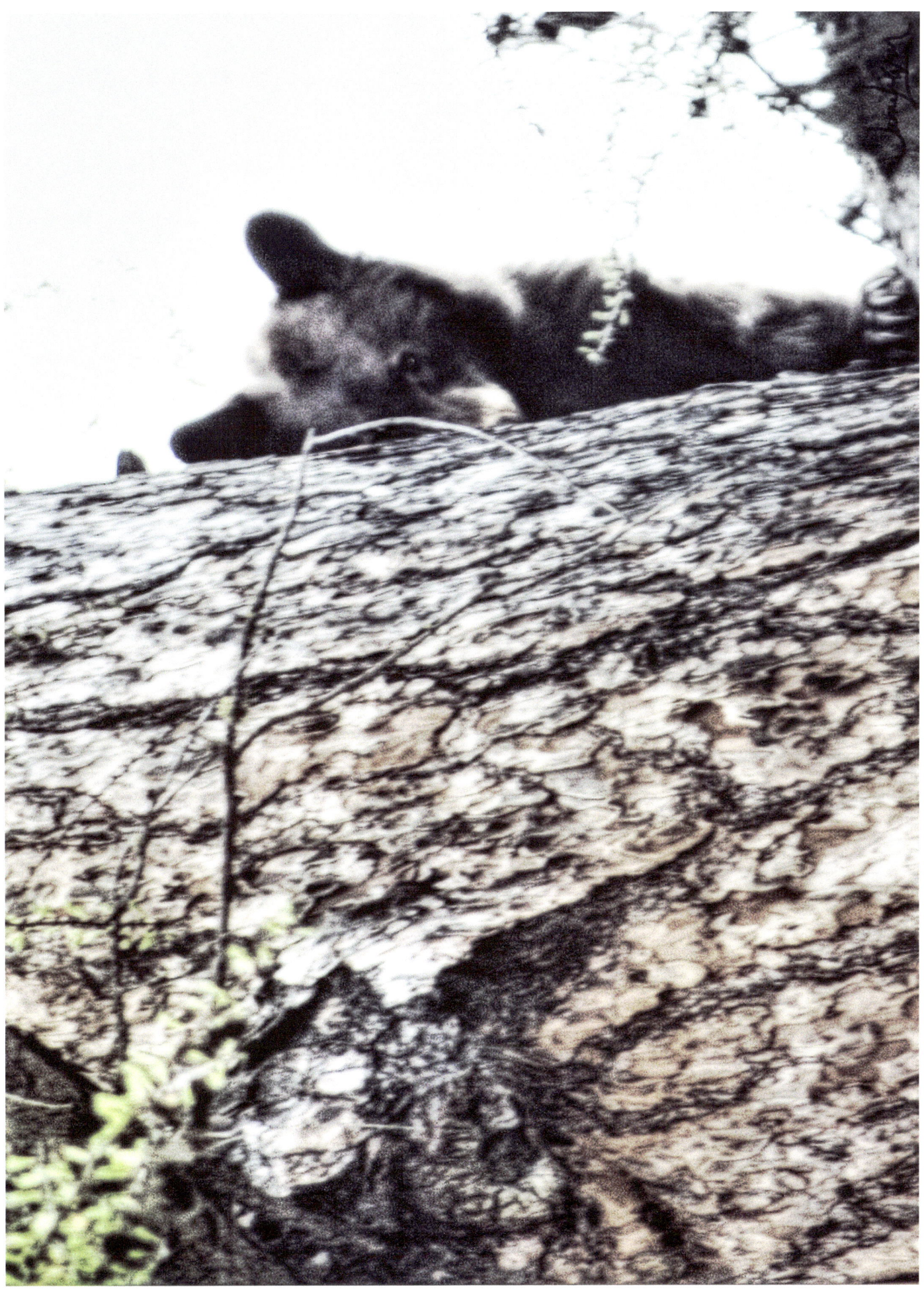

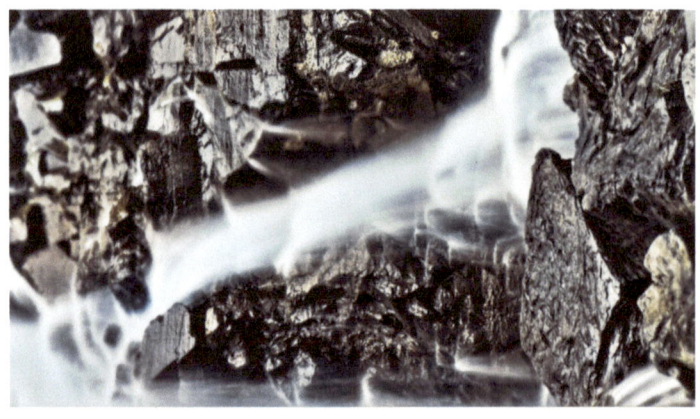
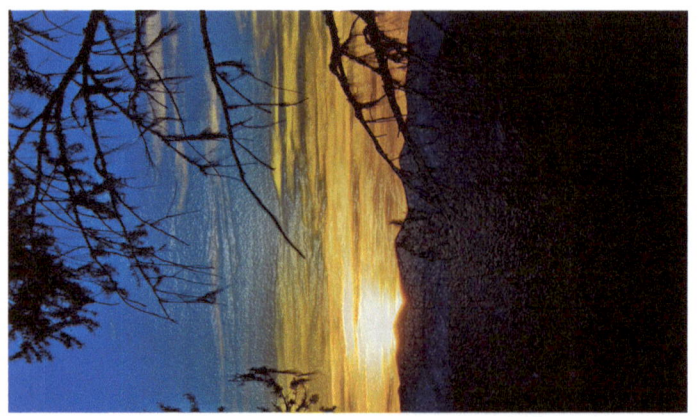
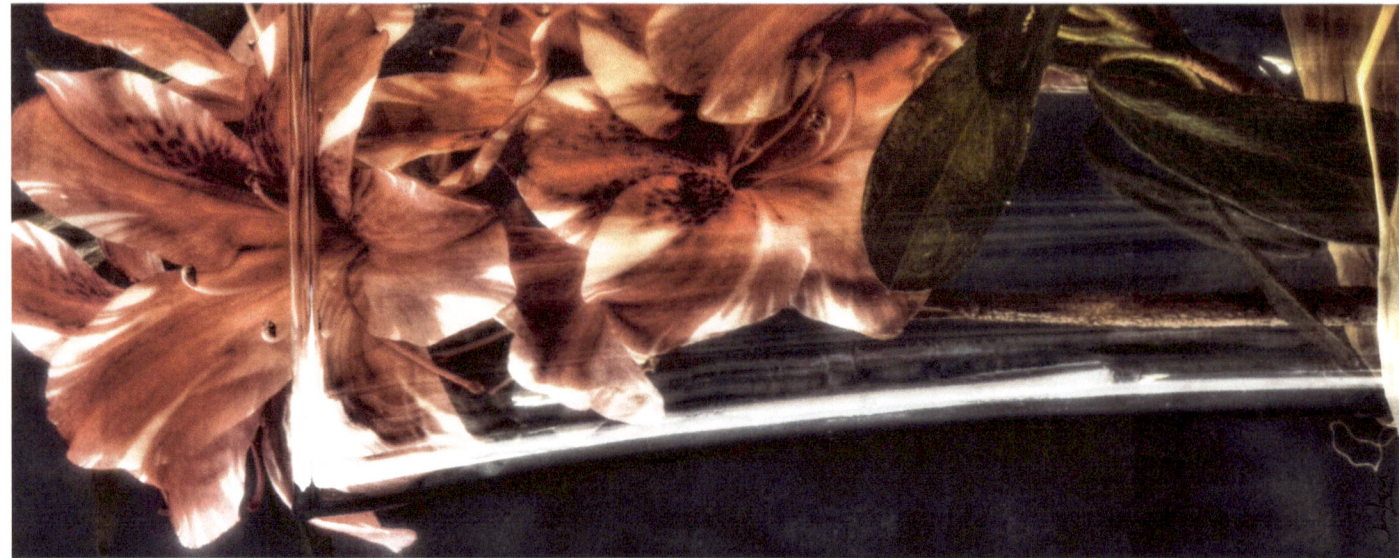
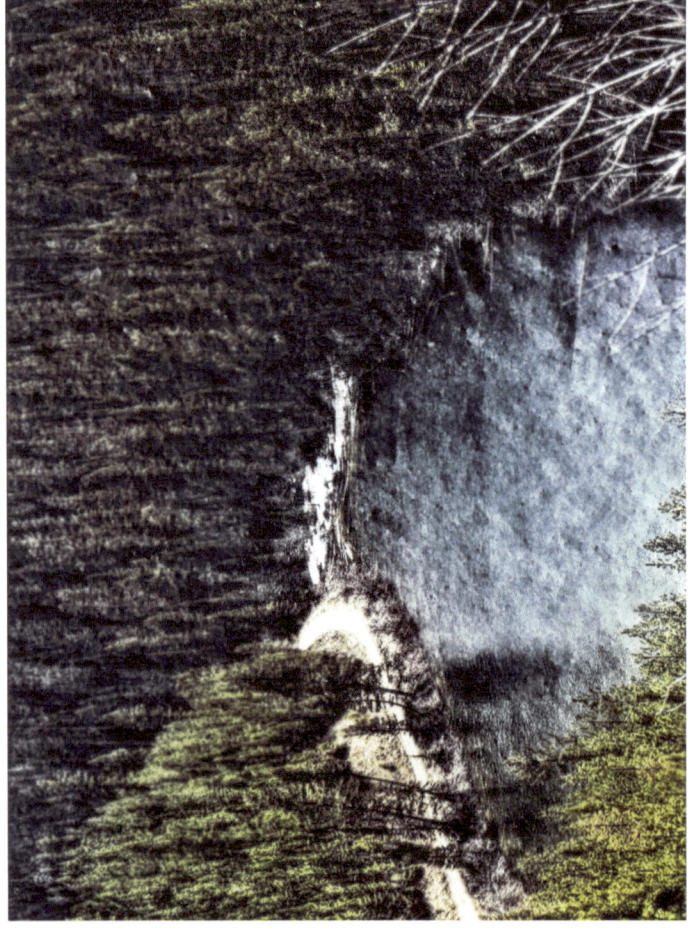
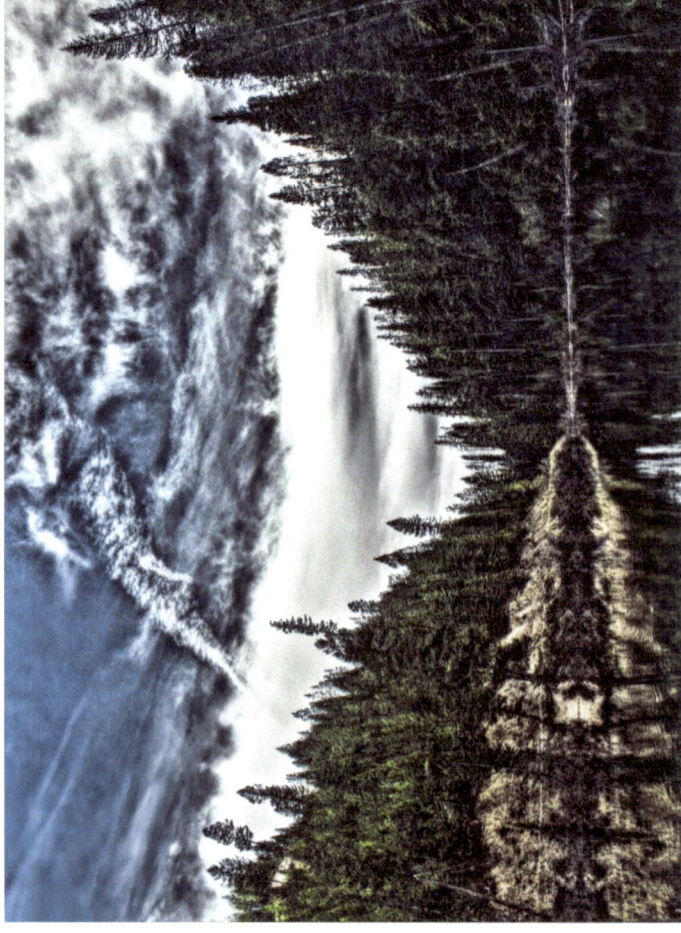

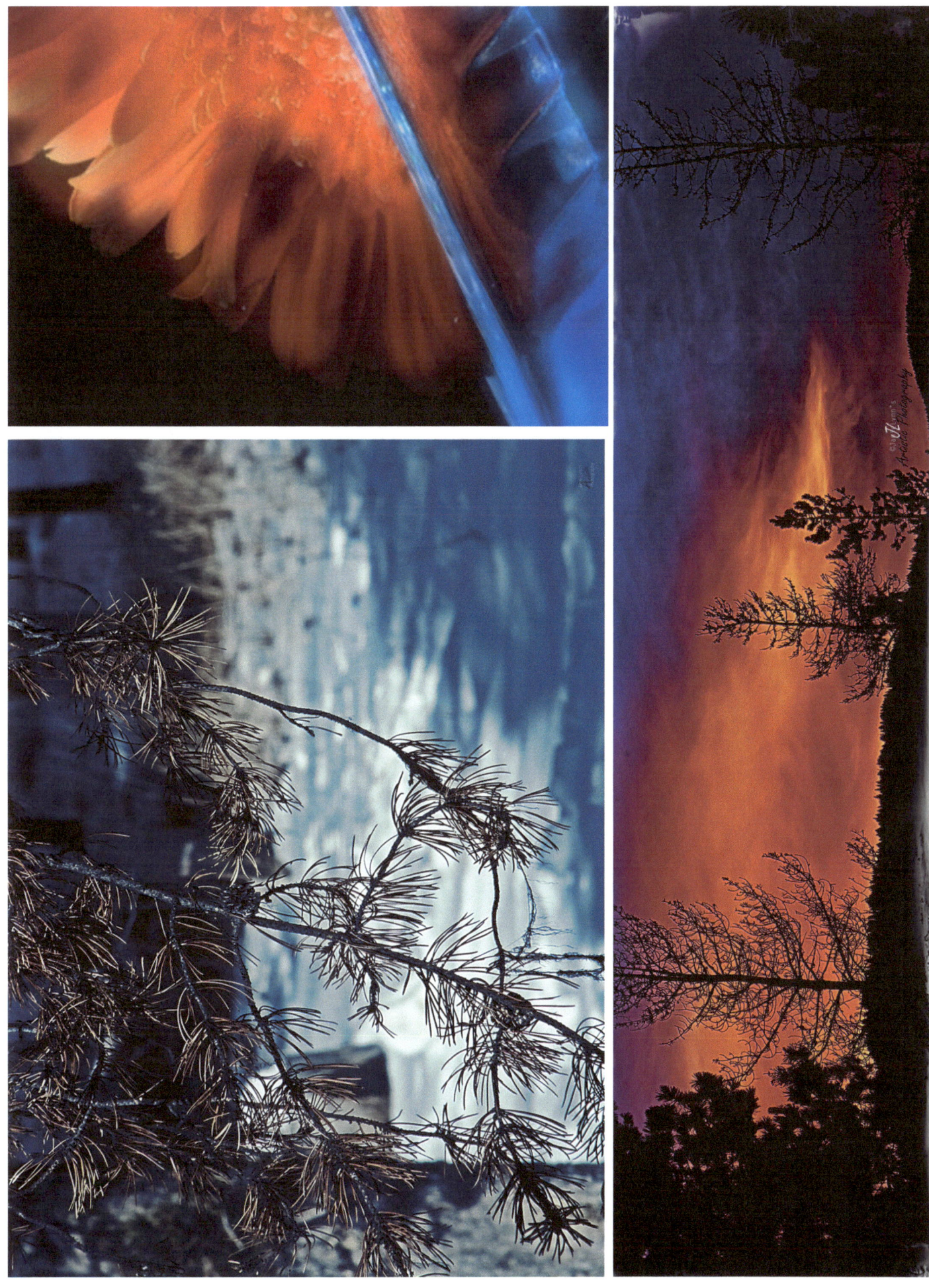

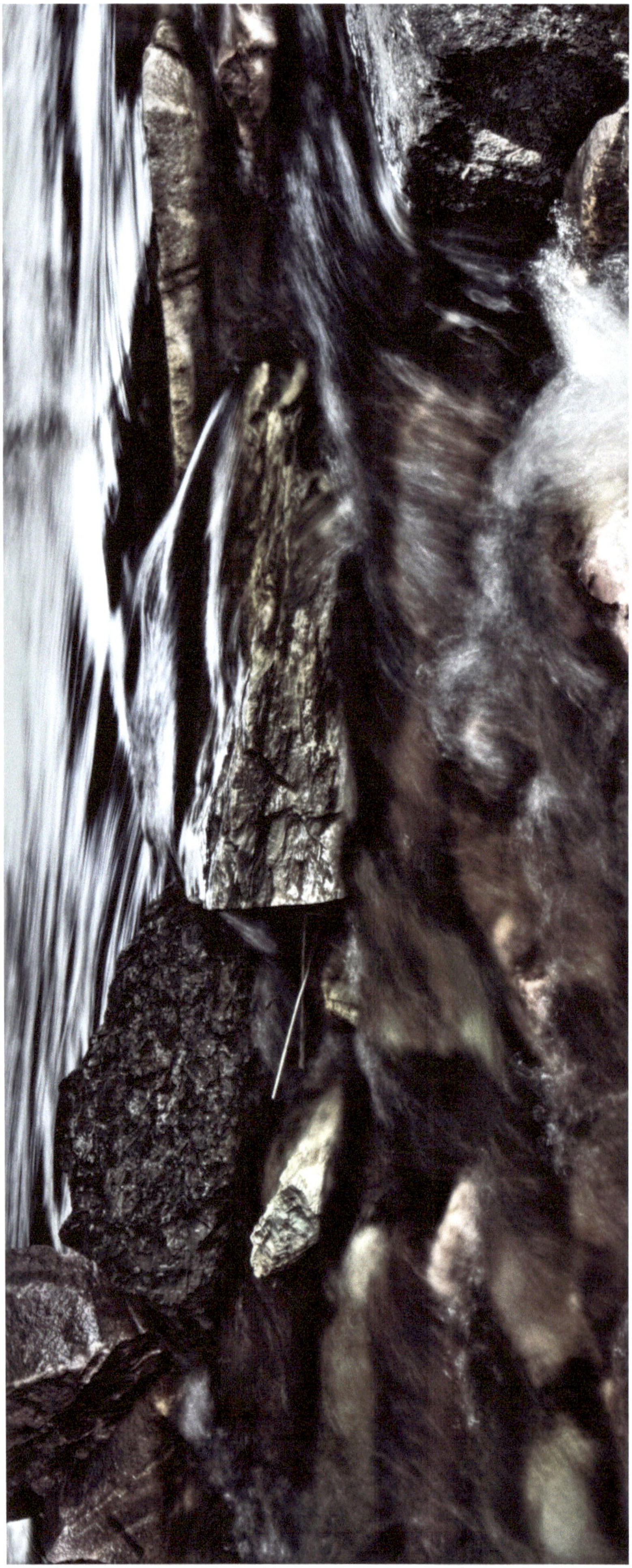

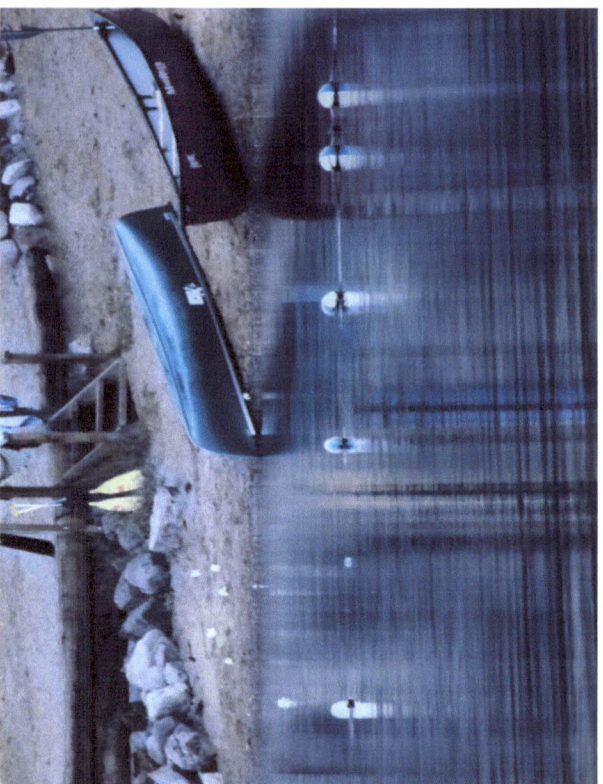
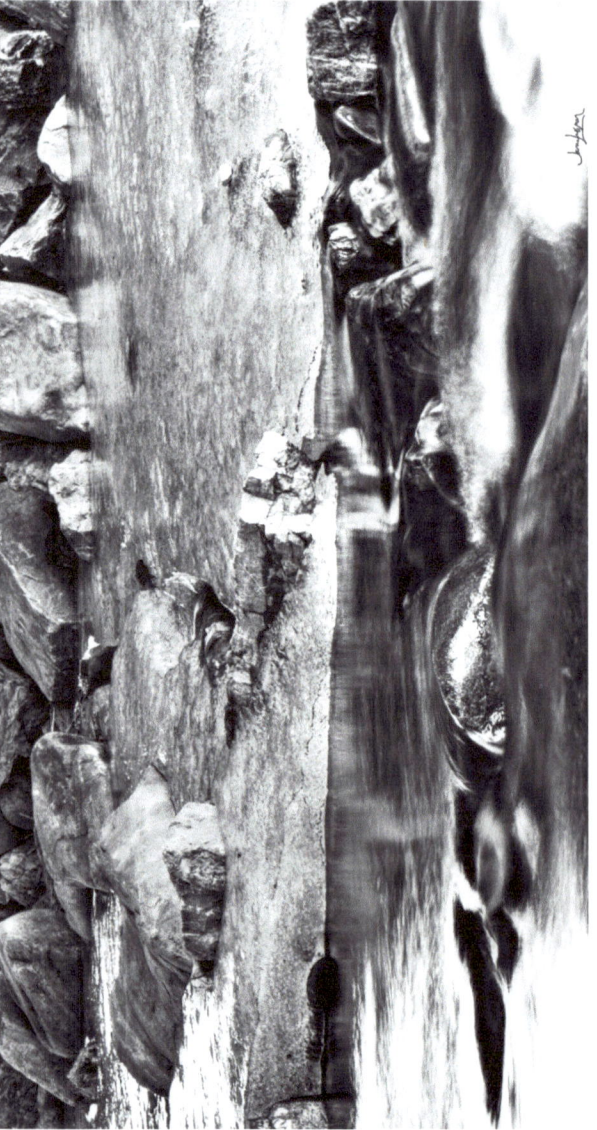

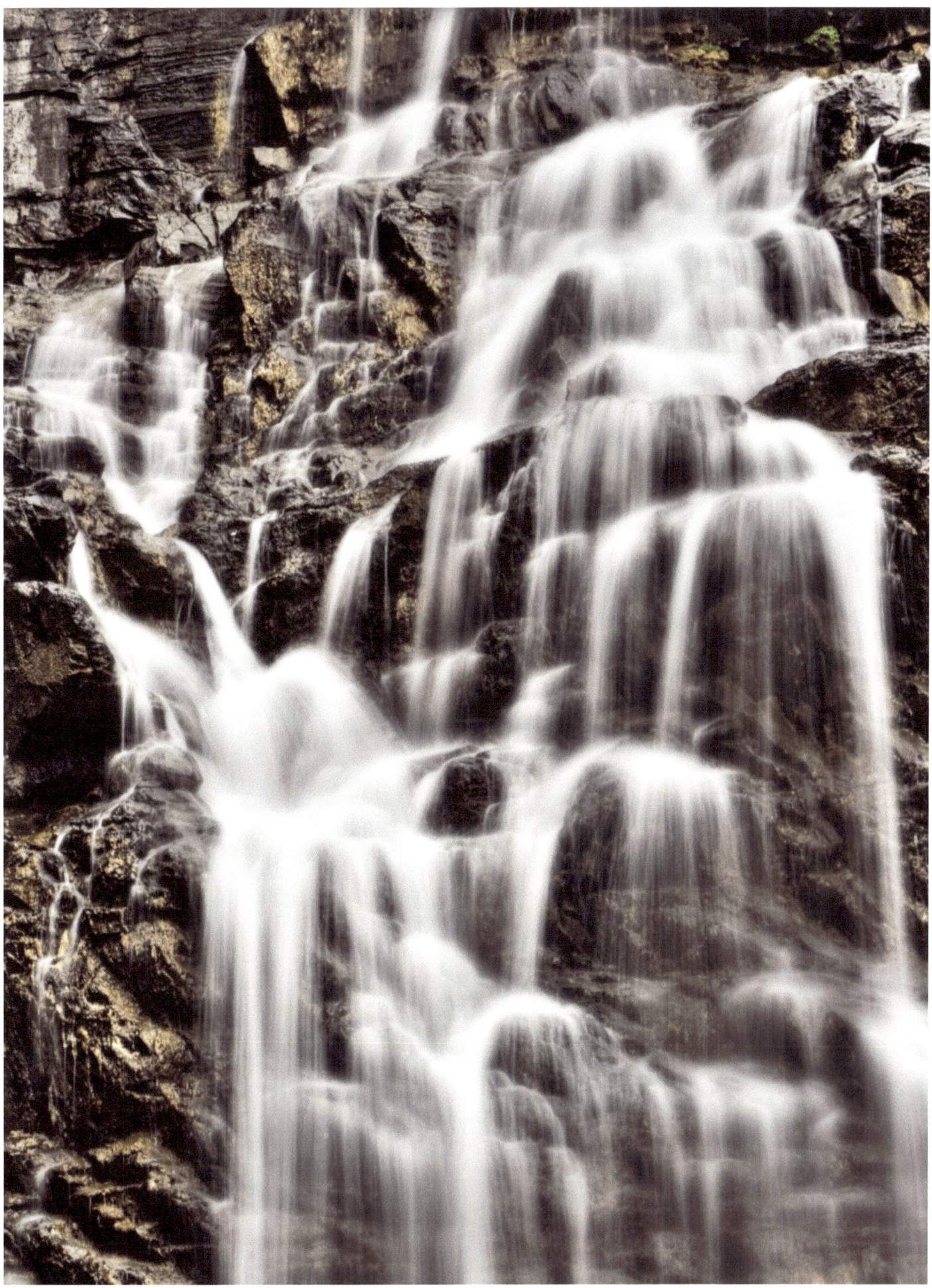

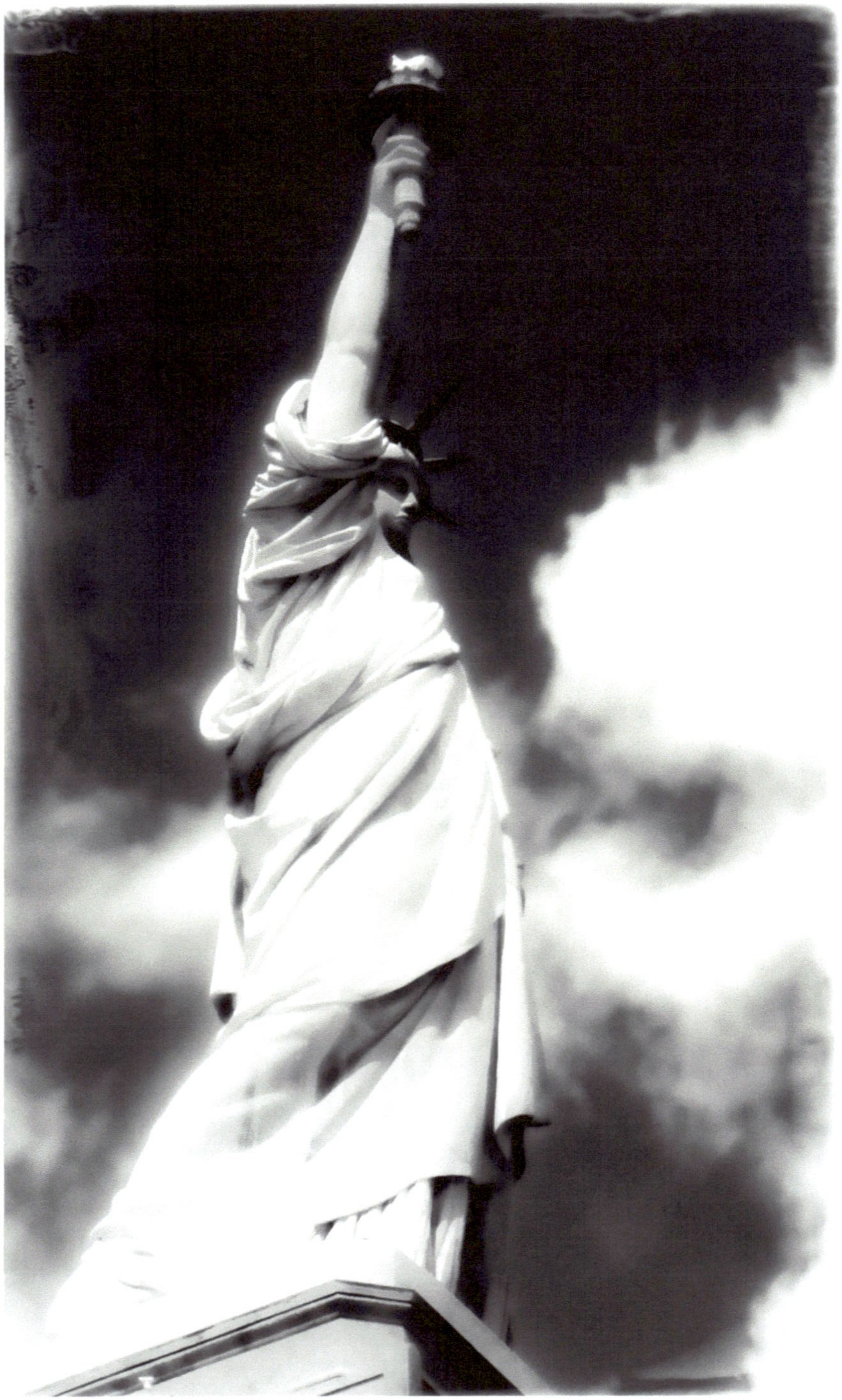

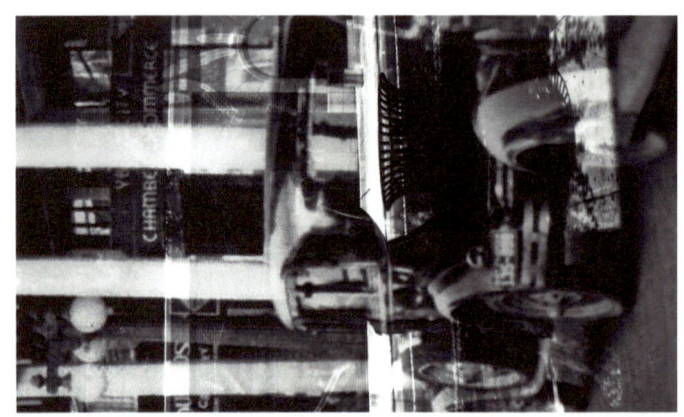
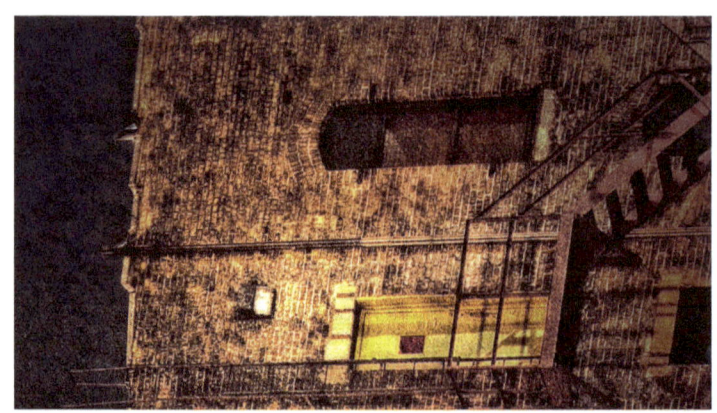
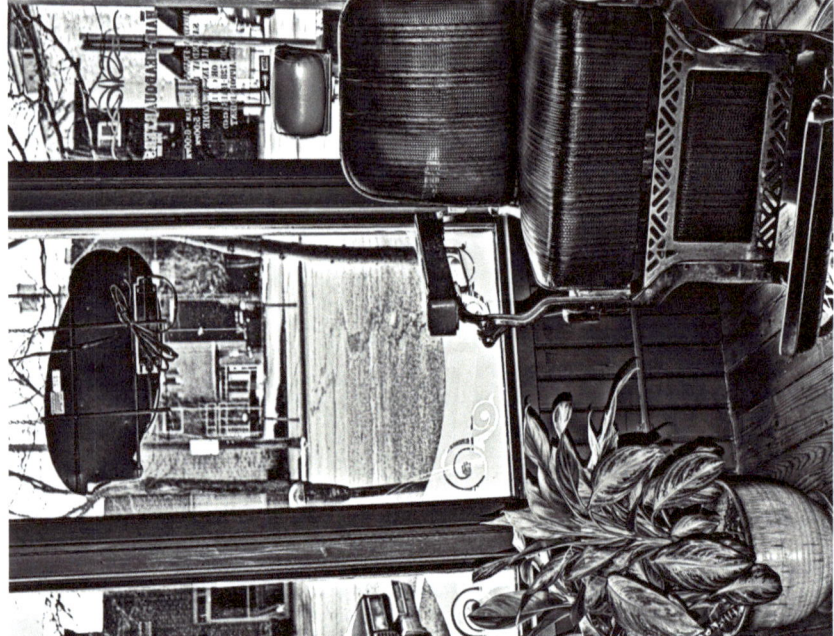
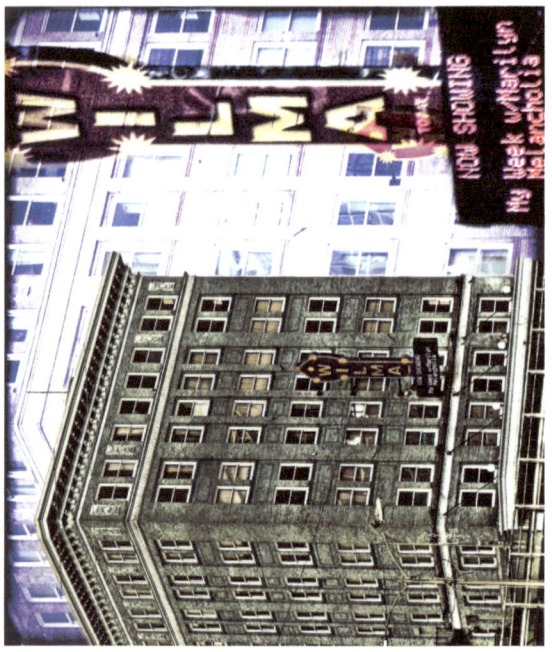

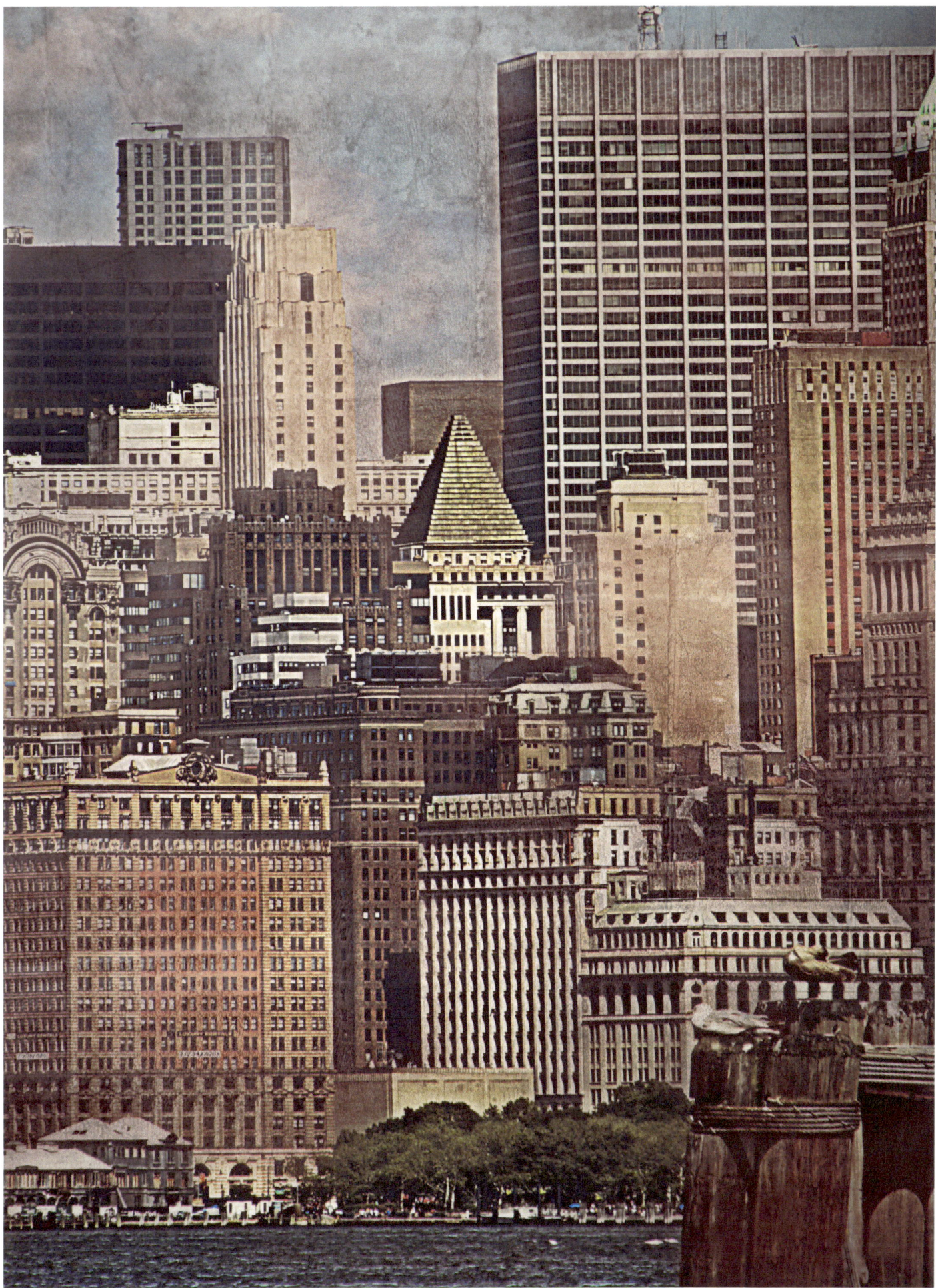

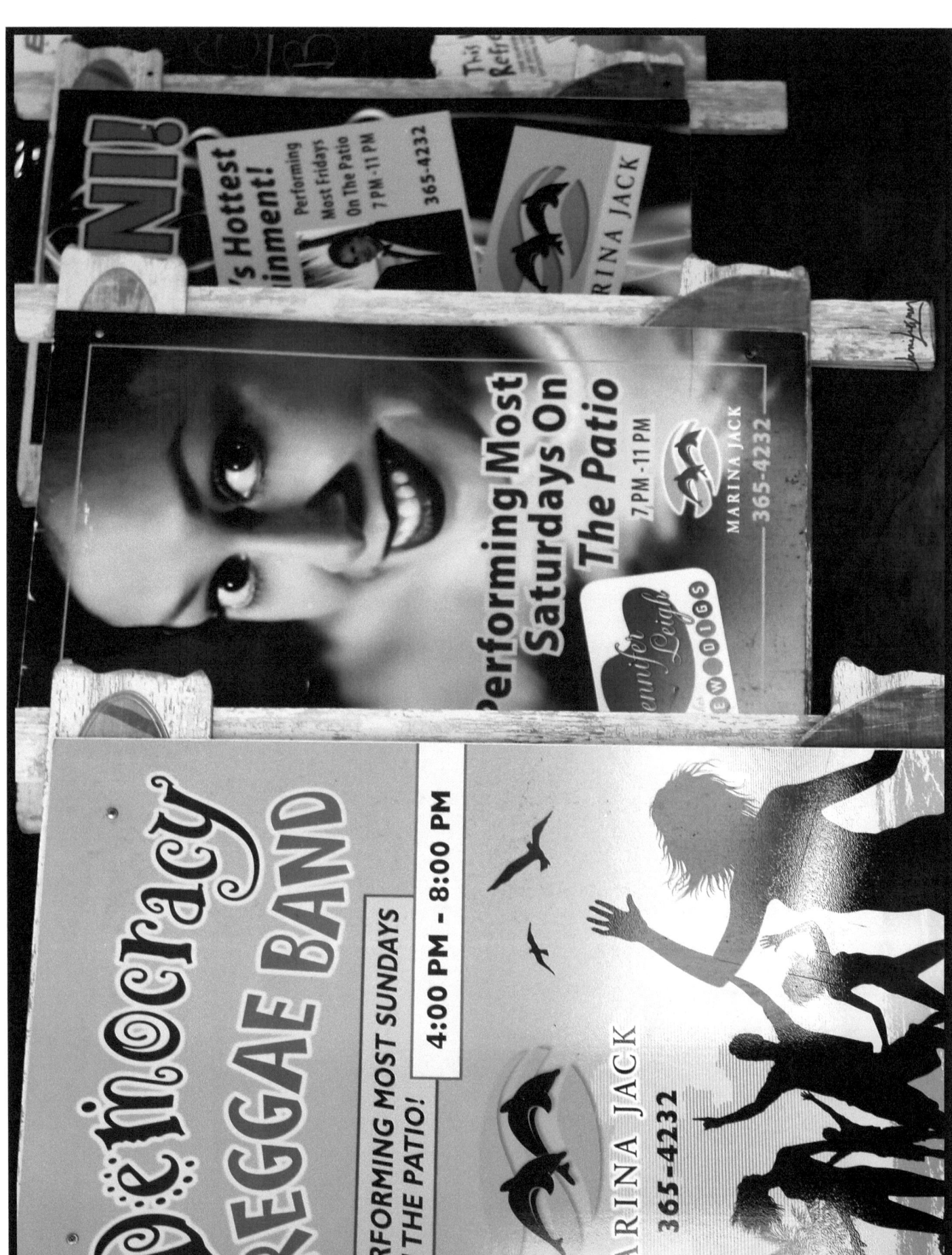

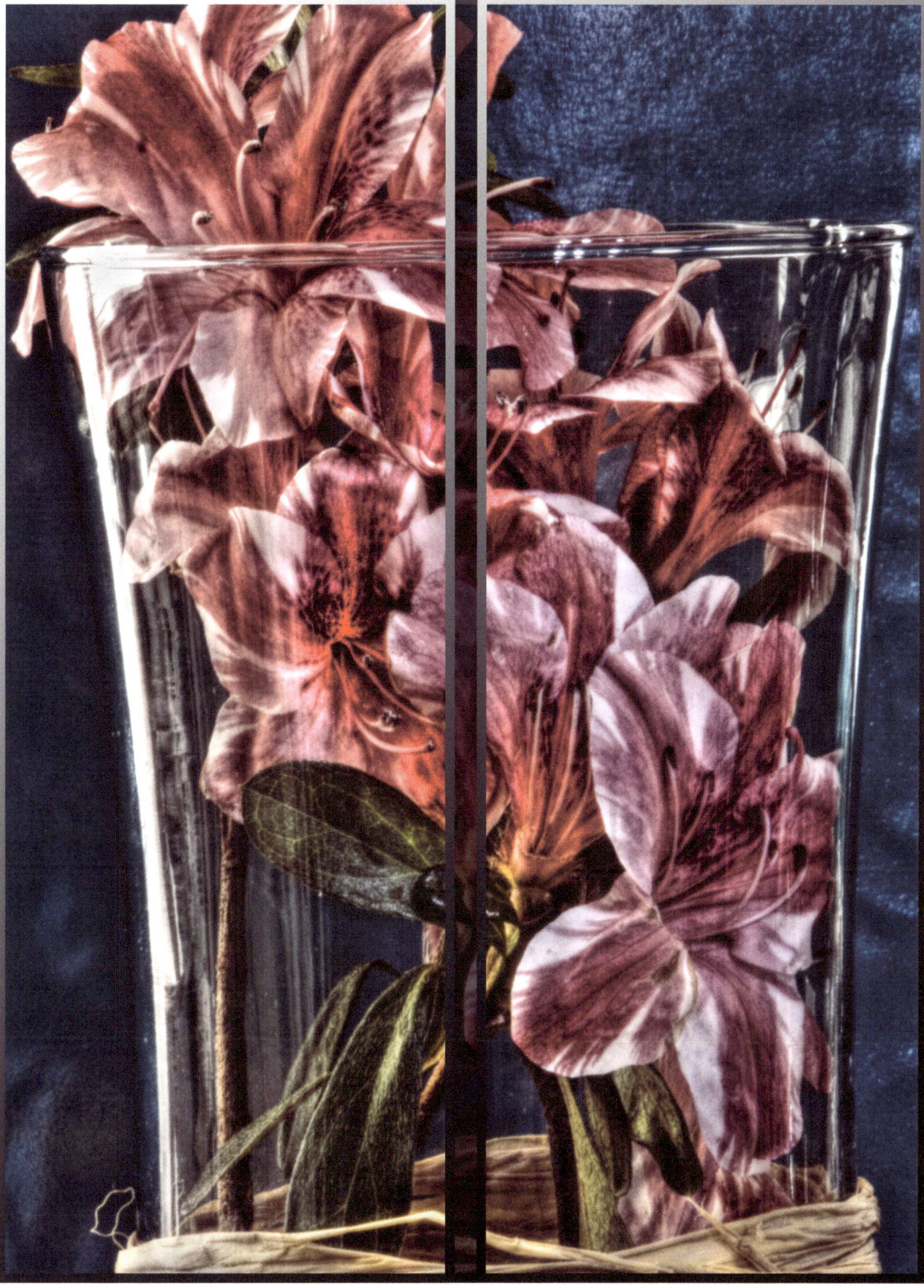

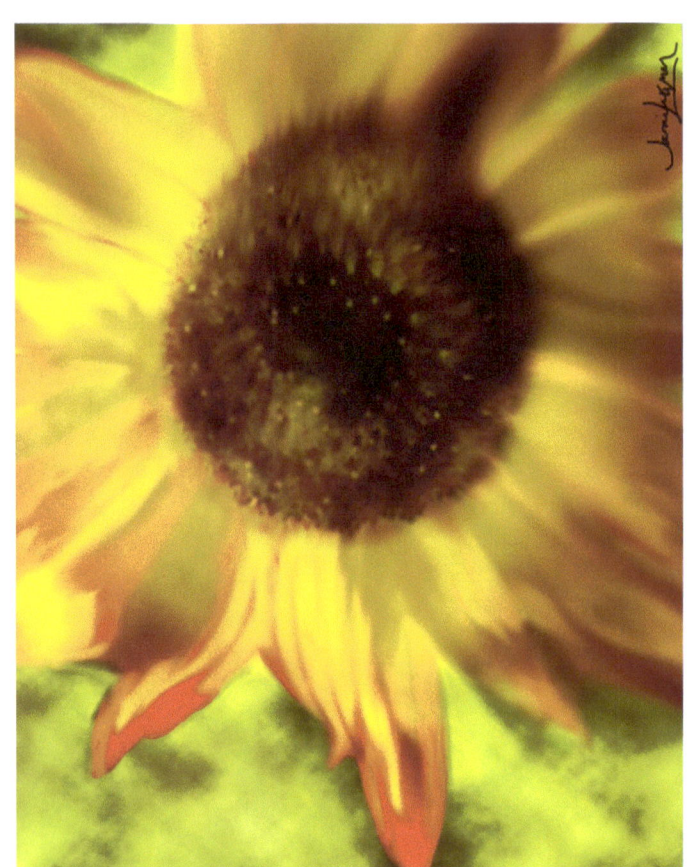

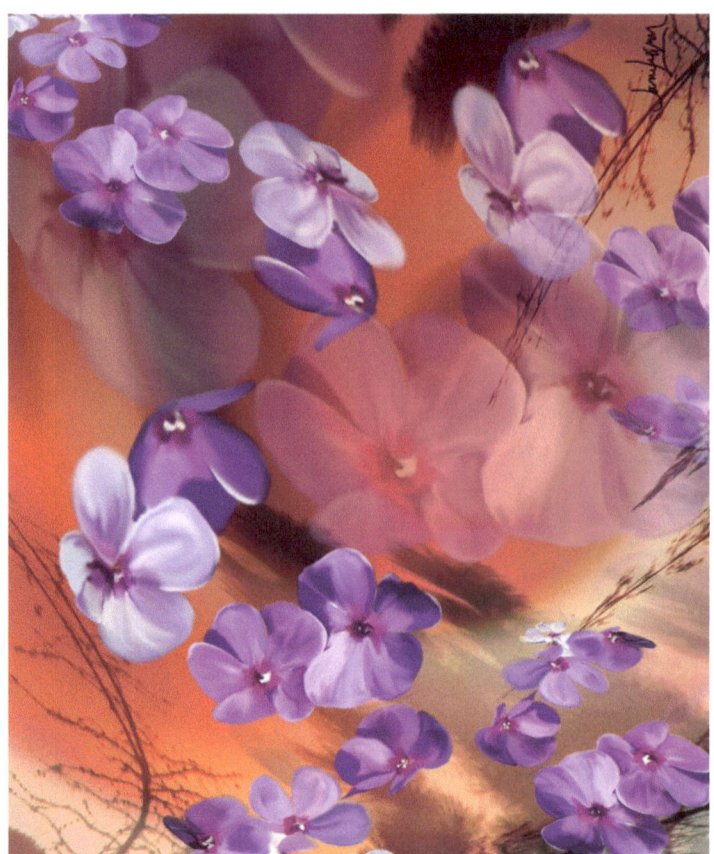

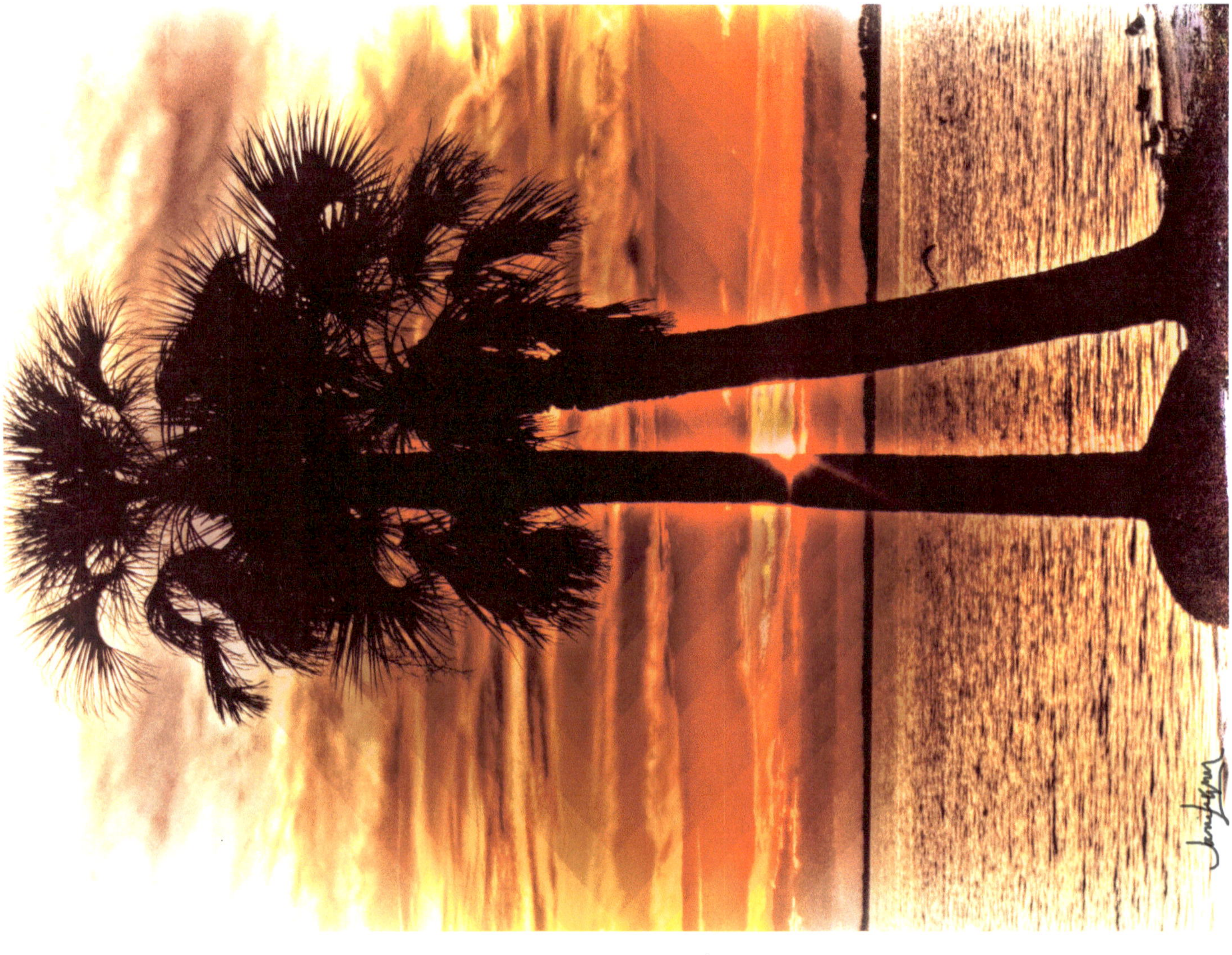

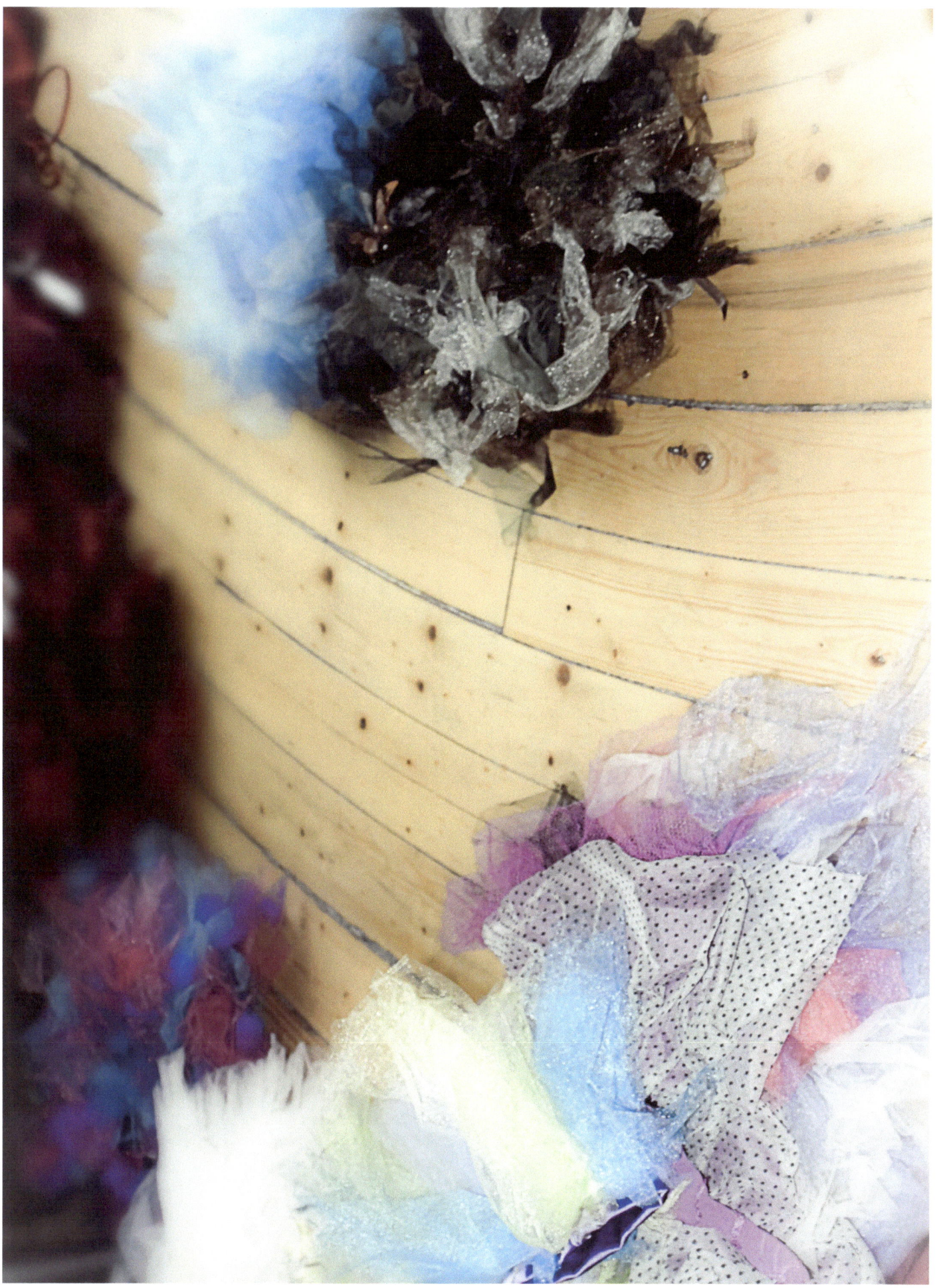

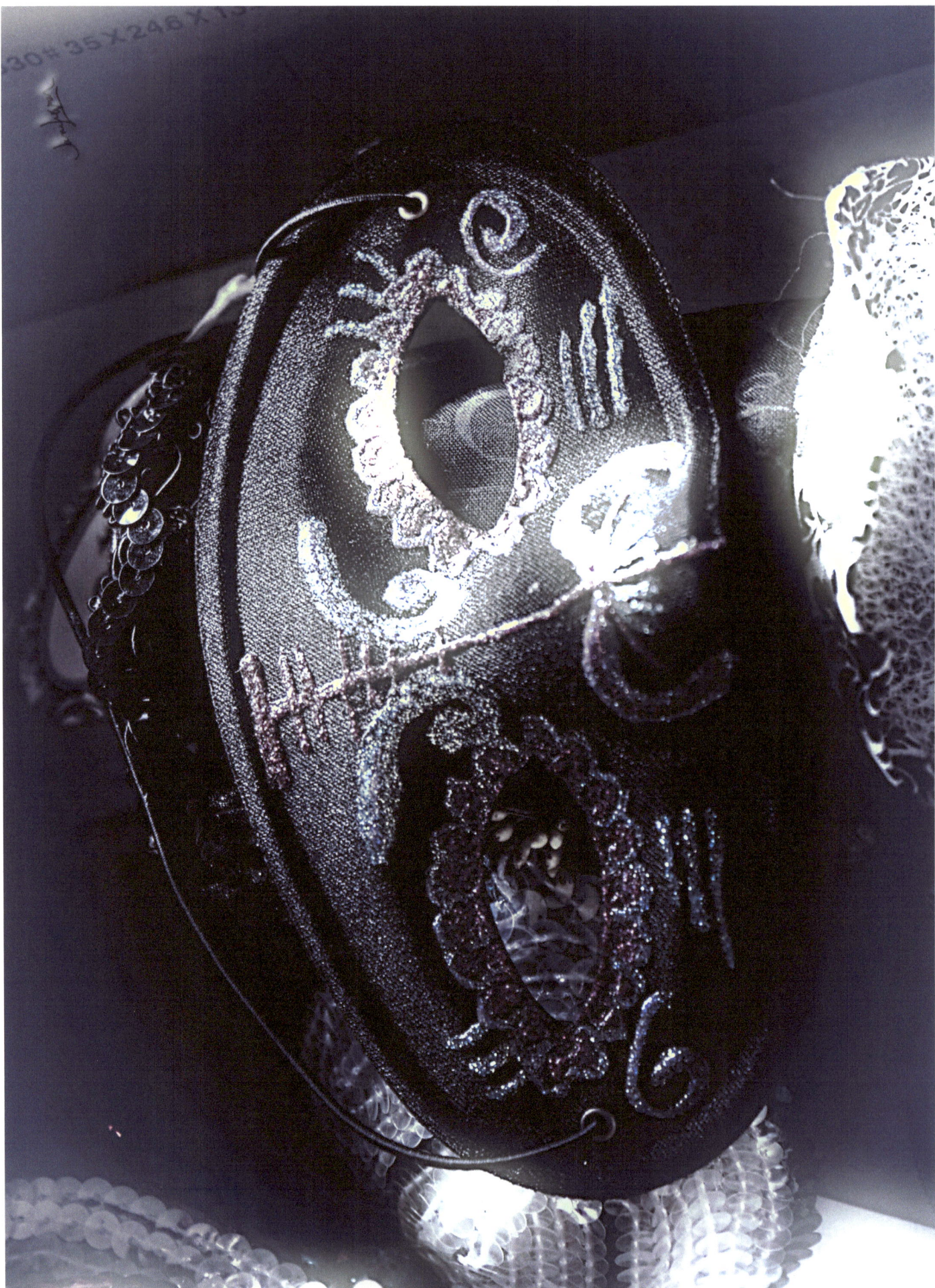

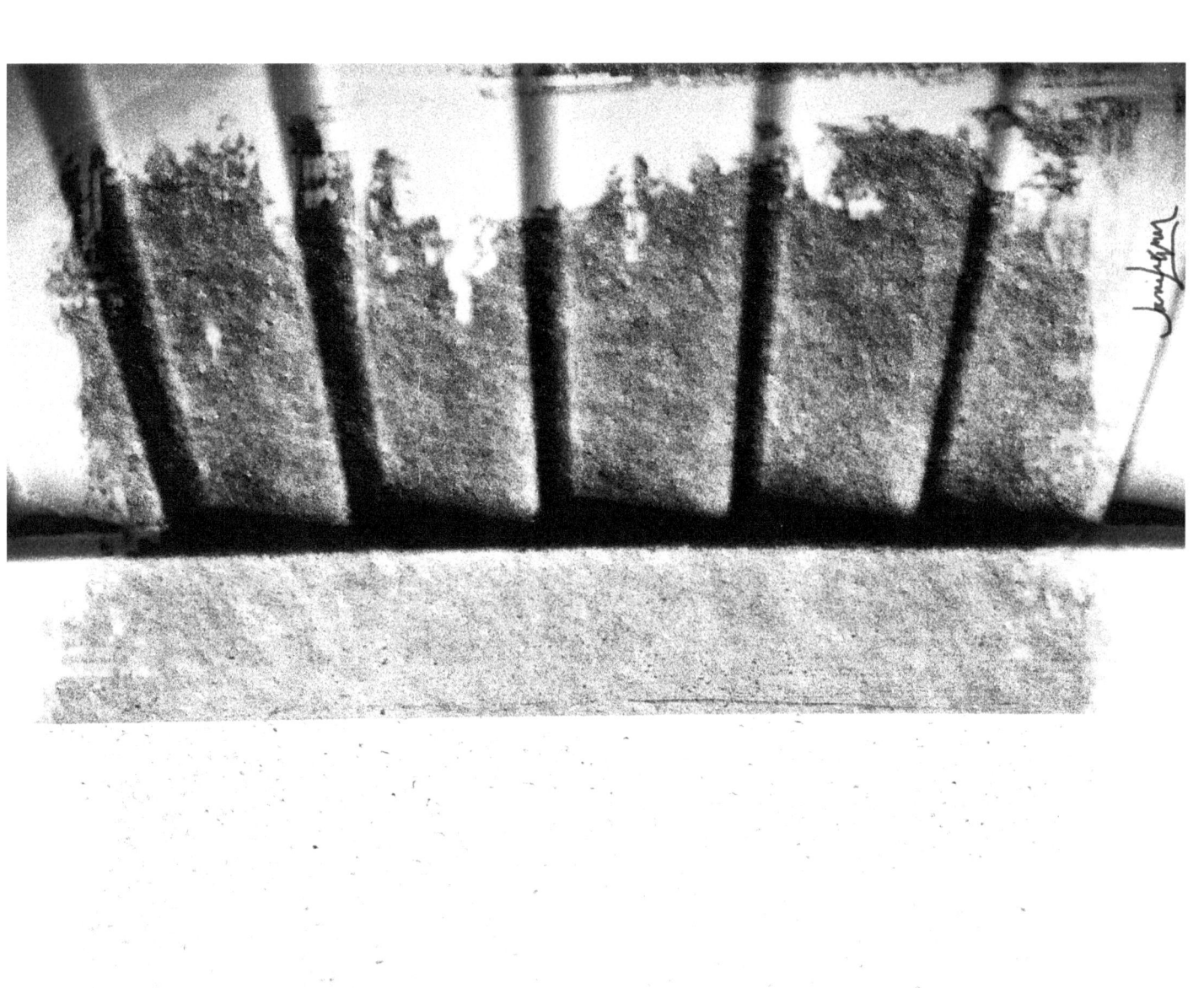